>>>

Write
On
Target

>>>

▶▶▶

Write On Target

▶▶▶

*A Five-Phase Program
for Nonfiction Writers*

▶▶▶

**Dennis E. Hensley
Holly G. Miller**

THE WRITER, INC.
Boston

Library of Congress Cataloging-in-Publication Data

Hensley, Dennis E., 1948-

Write on target: a five-phase program for nonfiction writers / by Dennis E. Hensley and Holly G. Miller.

p. cm.

ISBN 0-87116-177-X (pbk.)

1. Authorship.   I. Miller, Holly.   II. Title.

PN147.H376 1995   95-19050

808' .02--dc20   CIP

PRINTED IN THE UNITED STATES OF AMERICA

Contents

Phase One:
Preparing for a
Writing Career

Preparing for a Writing Career

"The discipline of the writer is to learn to be still and listen to what his subject has to tell him."

—Rachel Carson

Historically, people from all walks of life have given up their first calling to become writers of nonfiction. Jack London was a sailor and prospector before writing his social commentary, *The People of the Abyss*. Mark Twain had been a riverboat pilot and prospector before writing his observations of Americans in *The Innocents Abroad* and *Life on the Mississippi*. Ernest Hemingway was an ambulance driver and newspaper reporter before writing about bullfighting in *Death in the Afternoon*.

More recently we've seen James Herriot, a veterinarian, gain international acclaim for his nonfiction work *All Creatures Great and Small* and its sequels. Scott Turow was a lawyer who turned to writing nonfiction (*One L*) and fiction (*Presumed Innocent*), and Michael Crichton was trained as a medical doctor before he, too, started writing nonfiction (*Five Patients, Electronic Life*) and fiction (*Jurassic Park, Disclosure*).

Writers, it would seem, come from all walks of life, all known professions. What they have in common is a desire to see their work in print.

How do authors get to the top? And can others emulate their success and write bestsellers, too?

The answer to the first question is that they worked hard at mastering the craft of writing; they diligently sustained their output of written material for many years; and they continuously enhanced their writing professionalism by becoming experts at promoting themselves and their work.

The answer to the second question is, yes, similar success can be achieved by others. That is what this book is about: taking you through a five-phase program that will show you how to write professionally, sell your material, and manage your full- or part-time career as a free-lance writer.

Readers need new writers with new stories that are presented in new styles and new voices. And that's where *you* come in.

The procedures found in this book are not designed to make you a clone of any successful author now in print, but rather to enhance the creativity and depth of experiences already within you. For example, you will be shown the patterns that can be followed to come up with a memorable title or a gripping lead, but you will not be given a list of titles and leads that have already been used by someone else. The object is to teach you the processes by which you can create original works. After all, that is what will make you unique and successful as an author.

You have something else in your favor, too. This book offers you the combined experiences and insights of working editors, writers, columnists, and reviewers, in addition to lessons and exercises that have been tested, refined, and perfected over a ten-year period in college courses, writers' conferences, and writers' workshops. Any materials that students found particularly valuable in helping them master the process of writing are included—and they're yours for the taking.

When you are ready to progress to the next level of writing, this book will show you how to go about it. But be prepared to shed some old attitudes and beliefs as you develop your game plan for success. How you view your writing career has a great deal to do with the degree of success you will achieve.

Developing Your Game Plan for Success

Imagine this scenario.

A new business has opened in your neighborhood, and you have no way of knowing the nature of the business because the proprietor has neither advertised her services nor hung out a "shingle." Curious, you stop by during normal business hours—between 9 a.m. and 5 p.m.—but no one is there. However, you notice that the lights are on at unconventional times— late at night and on Saturdays and Sundays. You watch and you wait, and one day you manage to catch the owner when she is in the office. You mention that she keeps irregular hours. She replies that she works only when her creative juices are flowing. "Sometimes that's twelve hours at a stretch," she says, "and then I might burn out and not work for days."

You ask for a business card and brochure that explains her products and services. She shakes her head; sorry, she doesn't have any. You say you'd like to see a display of her work. She apologizes; she has no display.

You ask her what she makes.

When to Go Pro

I see my free-lance writing primarily as a:

_____ hobby to be enjoyed when and if time permits.

_____ source of "fun money" for me and my family.

_____ part-time revenue generator.

_____ major means of income.

I currently earn an average of $_____ per year from my writing.

As a full-time writer I'd need to make an annual salary of $_____.

My hourly rate for services is $_____.
        How to figure your hourly free-lance rate:
        1. Determine your target annual income $ _____.
        2. Add 25 percent for benefits $ _____.
        3. Add cost of overhead or expenses $ _____.
        4. Divide by the number of work hours $ _____.
           (30 hours per week X 48 weeks = 1,440 hours)
        5. Your hourly rate is $ _____.

Among the writing and writing-related services I can offer are:

___ Articles   ___ Ghostwriting   ___ Scripts
___ Annual reports   ___ Newsletters   ___ Speech writing
___ Brochures   ___ News releases   ___ Teaching
___ Company histories   ___ Nonfiction books   ___ Typing
___ Contest judging   ___ Proofreading   ___ Writer in residence
___ Editing manuscripts   ___ Resumes   ___ Workshops

Items to consider: Will you have a sliding rate scale depending on the client or on the service you are performing? Which services do you want to cultivate? Which services do you plan to drop as you become more successful? How will you balance long-term assignments (books) with quick income generators (brochures)? How can you ensure a steady but not impossible workload?

She asks you what you need.

"What do you charge?" you inquire.

"What's your budget?" she answers.

As incredible as this scenario seems, it accurately describes the way many writers work: They don't keep a disciplined schedule; they have no printed material that explains the variety of writing they do; and they have no portfolio that shows the range of their writing skills. They've never determined the scope of their services; instead, they prefer to let a client propose a project and then they decide whether they can pull it off. They have no fee structure or business plan; they've set no goals or objectives; and their financial "records" are scribbled on the backs of envelopes.

Yet, they want to be taken seriously. They insist they're *professionals*!

And, in a sense, they are. Unlike many businesses, a free-lance writing career requires little cash outlay, no formal organization, no diploma, no certification, no experience, no rented space, and no secretarial support. Indeed, you can launch a professional writing career if you have:

- Access to a typewriter or word processor
- Access to a photocopier
- Assorted sizes of envelopes
- Postage
- Stationery

But to *succeed* as a professional writer, you need one additional quality: an attitude. Until you think and act like a professional writer (even if you've never earned a byline), no one will take your writing seriously.

This is not to suggest that to succeed as a writer you must resign from your current job, invest in pricey sales brochures and a portfolio, and rent an office where you will spend 40 hours a week at a keyboard. Many writers balance full-time office jobs with part-time writing careers. They keep irregular hours, often work on weekends, and operate from corners of spare bedrooms. Only when the free-lance assignments become frequent and lucrative enough to equal the salaries of their "real" jobs can they embark on full-time writing careers. But they often consider themselves professional writers long before they give up their vocational juggling acts. They become professionals not when they achieve their first sales, but the moment they begin to take writing seriously.

Accept for a minute the premise that "professional writer" is a mental rather than a financial state. Now, review the writer's worksheet on the previous page and put a check mark next to the working level where you are, and another check mark at the level where you would someday like to be.

Work your way through the exercise, and once the worksheet is complete, you will have taken a giant step toward professionalism. You will have set your immediate career goal (the level you aspire to) and your hourly rate;

you will have focused on your writing specialties and determined your priorities.

Your game plan is beginning to take shape. The countdown is set for you to begin.

Ready, Set, Write!

You probably have been thinking about launching your career as a free lancer for a long time, perhaps even for years. But now you've taken a decisive step: You've set aside a specific time to read the opening section of this book. You've broken away from the thousands of "talking" writers who are "going to sit down and write a book one of these days." Such people are everywhere, even at writers conferences. (Call them "conference junkies"; they love to play author, but they never get much writing done.) You, however, are a working writer. You've begun to develop your game plan for success, and at this very moment you are busy studying your craft.

Indeed, you've been *ready* for a long time. But now, you are also ready to go to work: Your mind is set; your attitude is set. You've established as a professional goal the next level of your writing career.

The only task remaining is to write, and this book is designed to get you started. It uses a three-step teaching process you are probably familiar with: (a) explain; (b) demonstrate; and (c) practice.

That's exactly how you are going to learn to write and market your material. This book explains how you can master various aspects of professional writing (titles, leads, endings, etc.). It demonstrates how to follow the same procedures (with examples, models, and patterns). It asks you to give it a try (with practice exercises, quizzes, and writing drills), so you will be able to put to work immediately the new skills you've learned in each phase of your development. Not only will this reinforce the lessons, but it will also give you the confidence necessary in your quest to become a writer.

You've been ready to start for a long time.

Now you're set.

It's time to turn the page and begin to write.

Phase Two: Learning to Write Professionally

Learning to Write Professionally

"If you want to be a writer, write."
—Epictetus

The techniques and practices of professional writing are so consistent, they can be applied to fiction and nonfiction writing. Master the techniques, follow the practices, and you will be successful in almost every form of writing.

Consider for a moment some of the best-selling nonfiction books of the past several decades: *The Right Stuff* by Tom Wolfe, *In Cold Blood* by Truman Capote, *Fatal Vision* by Joe McGinness, and *Blood and Money* by Thomas Thompson. Although they are based on facts, these books had the same fast pace, dramatic tension, and elements of human interest found in novels. In fact, when Bob Woodward and Carl Bernstein wrote their nonfiction book about the Watergate conspiracy and the fall of the Nixon administration, they titled it *All the President's Men*, because the events so closely paralleled a novel by Robert Penn Warren titled *All the King's Men*.

The same is also true of many works of fiction. Numerous best-selling novels have developed a sense of verisimilitude—that "ring of truth"—by including facts, research, historical references, and other data usually found in works of nonfiction.

You must, therefore, recognize at the outset that writing of all types has some basic characteristics and similarities. Your goal is to become a writer, not a "label," i.e., "children's author" or "inspirational writer" or, even more specialized, "environmental writer."

Authors of fiction and nonfiction must master certain common elements:

● *Expanded vocabulary*—A thorough understanding of how to use language to its full range.

- *Structure*—Ability to organize both fiction and nonfiction in a logical and interesting pattern.
- *Dialogue*—Persons who are quoted must have realistic speech patterns that readers will accept as valid.
- *Pace*—A sense of forward momentum, a steady rhythm of words, and a sense of story progression that doesn't get bogged down in details.
- *Background*—Research skills to make a manuscript ring true while revealing basic facts and people's opinions.
- *Observations*—Powers of observation and a talent for description that convince readers they are witnessing the action as it is taking place.
- *Human analysis*—Ability to examine and understand what motivates people to do what they do.

In fiction and nonfiction, characters must be properly motivated; readers must have a strong emotional response to what they are reading; the writing must show, not tell; and the sensory elements of a scene must be conveyed to readers through the colors, noises, aromas, and tactile sensations of that setting.

Too often, nonfiction writers don't understand the value—the necessity—of using fiction writing techniques to make nonfiction more acceptable. Nonfiction writing is not just a list of facts. No one can rationalize a boring article by saying, "But that's what really happened." That may be so, but if it's boring it won't sell. People want the stories behind the main story. Nonfiction writing needs the verve, drive, tone, flavor, and excitement of fiction. In writing nonfiction, writers may have all the facts, but they must give them shape to catch and hold the reader.

Getting the Right Ideas

Working writers are skeptical of aspiring authors who say they have difficulty coming up with bright ideas for articles and books. Instead of suffering from a shortage of ideas and topics, most established writers grumble that they can't turn off the idea spigot. The flow is so constant that unless the ideas are poured into a journal, they will be washed away by the next wave of creativity.

A frequent speaker at writers' conferences tells of a workshop that took place in the Bible Belt. Participants included talented regional writers who were convinced they couldn't break into national print unless they moved to New York City or Los Angeles.

"Ideas are everywhere—no matter where you live, regardless of what you do," the instructor assured the roomful of skeptics. "Some of the best material is right in your own back yard, but you may not recognize it because you're so close to it."

Many pupils shook their heads in disagreement. "We can tell that you've never lived in these parts!" challenged one woman. "Don't misunderstand us: This is home, and we love it, but there's nothing going on here that would interest an East Coast magazine editor."

The instructor urged them to brainstorm. They did, and drew a blank. She tried to stimulate their creativity by asking questions: What about local history? Any famous folk born in the area? Interesting landmarks? People with unusual occupations or hobbies? Colorful characters pursuing crazy dreams? The last question caused a slight stir in the audience.

"Well, there's that fella up north who built the monastery," ventured a voice. They seemed well acquainted with the story.

"Let me in on it," prodded the teacher. "Tell me more."

"Beautiful facility," someone responded. "It's got a gym, cafeteria, dorms. . . . The only problem is, the whole elaborate place has just one monk—the same guy who built it. Of course, he's tried to attract others; even ran an ad in *The New York Times,* but I don't think he had any takers."

The instructor was fascinated by the bizarre anecdote and pointed out the many directions the story could take. Spend a day working side by side with this man, she suggested. Ask him all the questions that readers might ask: "Why are you doing this?" "Where did you get the funds?" "What responses did your ad generate?"

Or, plan a round-up article and talk with several people who lead solitary lives—a lighthouse keeper, the caretaker at a closed summer resort, a former political prisoner. Ask logical questions: "How do you fill your days?" "How do you deal with loneliness?" "Which aspects of solitary living do you like?" "Which aspects are difficult for you?"

Or, write a motivational article about people who overcome great odds to make their dreams come true. Find an entrepreneur who launched a multi-million-dollar business on a $50 loan; a great-grandmother who learned to fly in spite of her age; a blind law student who earned the highest score on the state bar exam. Feature the monk and his monastery in a sidebar.

The teacher's enthusiasm was catching. Within three months she received a full-page newspaper clipping from one of the workshop participants. The writer had interviewed the monk, written a detailed profile, sold it to one of the state's largest dailies, and was in the process of sending out query letters to national magazines.

Developing idea awareness

The key to locating marketable ideas is awareness. You can boost yours in several ways: by listening to people communicate, by reading a variety of publications, by listening to radio and television talk shows, and by following the news. Good writers are good listeners. They listen to talk on the radio, eavesdrop on cocktail party conversation, interview retirees who like to spout wisdom from park benches, and listen to Sunday sermons. They learn to gauge the audience's response to a topic by distinguishing between polite attention and passionate interest. They also spend a lot of time reading newspapers as diverse as *The Wall Street Journal* and *USA Today,* specialty as well as general-interest magazines, such as *Industry Week* and *The Saturday Evening Post,* and, of course, books. They selectively watch television and films, and listen to audio tapes in the tape decks of their cars.

Many writers describe themselves as news junkies who are naturally curious and are always receiving and storing information. They're "clip artists" who can't read their daily newspapers without scissors in hand. Whenever they come across an interesting fact or anecdote, they clip and file it by topic in "tickler files," which are really informal idea banks. From time to time, writers sort through these files, discarding some, refiling others, and when several clips seem loosely related to the same topic, they create a separate folder for a new subject. Folders that began with a single item clipped from a local newspaper often lead to articles and books.

What interests you?

The old advice that writers should write about subjects that interest them has validity—especially for beginning authors. (Experienced writers typically write what editors assign them.) If you are a beginner, make a list of topics that you find fascinating and would like to learn more about. To help you create the list, ask yourself what types of articles and stories attract you. Do you automatically reach for the sports section of the Sunday newspaper first? The financial report? Items about health and fitness? Crime reports? Opinion pieces? The arts? You should probably write the type of article that you like to read.

Take the exercise one step further. Imagine that you're holding your TV's remote control and you're scanning the channels. What programs are you likely to watch? Situation comedies? Historical documentaries? Interviews with well-known personalities? A series on the environment? Reading voluminous background material, conducting interviews, and writing numerous drafts will be far more enjoyable if your subject is one that excites you.

As you take inventory of your interests, try to recall topics that intrigued you as a child or a young adult. Chances are, they still hold a certain allure. Don't be surprised if a subject that interested you 10 or 20 years ago suddenly resurfaces as the basis of a book or an article. Some ideas require long incubation periods.

Watch out for crossroads

As you scout for ideas, be aware of life's crossroads—those key points at which people tend to take off in new directions: transitions from high

Looking for Bright Ideas?

Having trouble coming up with unusual article ideas? Try these exercises to nudge your creativity.

1. Visit the periodicals room of your library. Read the table of contents of several magazines (don't limit yourself to your favorite publications). How many of the articles cover topics that you could have researched and written about? What important topics have been overlooked? Make a list. This will be your starting point for an "idea file."

2. Check your local newspaper for human-interest items on colorful people engaged in interesting hobbies and activities. Note any conventions and professional meetings that will bring dozens of experts to town. Don't overlook the classified section that may promote everything from Elvis sound-alikes to rare books.

3. Get your state's map out of the glove compartment and draw a circle around your hometown. Look at all the attractions within a 50-mile radius. Bypass the obvious museums, theme parks, and state forests. Concentrate on the great Italian restaurant that is known only to local residents, the renovated movie house with the grand ballroom, the historic stop on the underground railroad. Now, grab your camera and take a little field trip.

4. Turn your calendar ahead six months (remember that magazines work from three to six months in advance) and take note of what's coming up. Prom party ideas? Antique gifts for the June bride?

5. Create a list of at least 20 well-known people from different walks of life (television, religion, politics, film, literature, business). Now think of one simple question or request that you would like to pose to all of them—"Who was the greatest influence in your life and why?" "What book had the most profound effect on you and why?" "Share your favorite holiday memory." "Share your favorite holiday recipe." Make your request in a letter and include a self-addressed, stamped envelope for a reply. Combine the responses into one article. If you don't receive enough answers (you'll need at least five), send out another round of the same questions to different personalities.

6. Don't reinvent the wheel! Look at one of your published articles (or a manuscript that has been rejected). Apply the four R's—Reslant, Revise, Review, Resell—and consider ways to produce a new version.

school to college, from college to the world of work, from single status to marriage, from life as a twosome to parenthood, from working to retirement, from marriage to widowhood or divorce. Readers need help with many of the dilemmas and decisions inherent in these pivotal points.

When you are looking for ideas you need to keep current with trends and also try to anticipate the implications of the trends. For example, the phenomenon of older Americans going back to college as "non-traditional students" is well documented. However, the creative writer looks beyond the trend and asks "what if" questions: What will happen to college life if campuses are taken over by older students whose day doesn't begin until after 5 p.m.? What will happen if 21-year-old graduates are pitted against their 40-year-old classmates in the job market? How is the college classroom environment affected by the presence of older students—from the points of view of the professors, other students? How do learning styles vary among age groups?

If you are struggling to find fresh ideas to pursue in your writing, review the exercise on the previous page. Choose an assignment that captures your interest, and then work until you have a single, well-developed topic. Determine the kind of research you will need to do by reading the next section of this book. Conduct just enough research to enable you to approach an editor with an enthusiastic query letter.

Painless Research

Mention the word "research" and most people stifle a yawn as they conjure up memories of term papers, dusty library stacks, bibliographies, footnotes, and the mystical duo of *ibid.* and *op. cit.*

Good news: Conducting research for free-lance writing and gathering data for college composition class bear little resemblance. You'll spend time at the library in both cases, but when you write for publication, you're interested not only in what *has* been published but also in what *has not* been published about your topic. Published material helps you understand your subject, but your goal is never to restate what is already in print. In reviewing published sources, your goal is to become so familiar with the topic that you will be able to discover previously unknown information.

Bad news: Some research is necessary for almost every writing project you undertake. If you don't spend enough time gathering information from a variety of sources, you can write only from personal experiences and about topics you already know well. For most people, that translates into a very short writing career. So, like it or not, you'll need to acquire and hone research skills. You may find that research will become your favorite part of the writing process.

The local library is almost always the first and best launching point. A few minutes at the library's computer can help you decide if the topic you're anxious to tackle is original. Type in your key words and note the number of citations that come on the screen. If it is a long list you may opt not to add to the glut of information. A short list is a good sign! It could be an idea whose time has come—not come and gone.

By reviewing several published articles, you may determine that your chosen subject is larger than you thought. Do you need to take a tighter focus than you originally planned? Is the topic too broad for an article? Could it be better handled as a series of articles? As a book?

Library research will help you identify sources you might want to contact, so look for names of people frequently quoted as "experts." These often are people who themselves have written books and articles about the subject. Where are they located? Who are their publishers? How can they be reached?

Library research also will indicate if you can afford to take on a writing project. Remember, every nonfiction book or article carries a price tag. At some point—the earlier the better—you need to determine how much it will cost you to produce a finished manuscript. How many long-distance phone calls will be involved? How many out-of-town trips? What are you likely to earn for this piece of writing? Will you be able to resell it? Does it have potential for long "shelf life" or is it so timely that you won't be able to recycle the information in other ways to other editors? (See discussion of multiple marketing in Phase Four.)

To understand the forms that research can take *beyond* your trip to the library, review the legwork that went into three assignments, two for magazine articles and one for a book.

• For a feature about one of the top collecting hobbies in America— dolls and figurines—one writer scheduled a shopping trip after her visit to the library. She needed to see and touch what she had read about in the collectibles journals. She poked around gift boutiques, antique stores, and toy shops. She became familiar with the names of popular doll designers, the prices that certain models could command, and she learned the criteria for judging dolls. This facet of in-store research led to a more expanded opportunity when a shopkeeper gave her a brochure promoting an upcoming doll show. She attended and met dozens of collectors who happily shared their expertise via impromptu interviews.

• Another author, who was gathering research for a book based in Detroit, spent a couple of days walking the streets of the city. He needed to familiarize himself with the affluent old neighborhood where his key figure had lived, to learn the names of restaurants the person patronized, the radio station he listened to, and the newspaper he read. If the author was to recreate his character's drive to work each morning accurately, he needed to know traffic patterns, distances between points and landmarks along the way. These were details that only on-site research could provide.

• A travel writer who wanted to write about Norway's Winter Olympics arranged to fly to Oslo, take a train to Lillehammer and visit the ski jumps, the hockey arena, luge track, and other Olympic sites. She took notes, snapped pictures, and ate reindeer meat—all in the name of research. (Not all research is that glamorous!)

Most writers engage in four kinds of research: library, observation, participation, and interviews. Every project is different and may not require all four varieties, although most writing assignments involve some combination of the four. Often an author will approach research in this order:

Library—Make copies of the best published articles you can find. As you read through the material, jot down questions that come to mind but are not answered in the text. Vow to find the answers. Underline the names of persons you might want to track down for interviews. Use a highlighter to emphasize pertinent facts that you might want to include in your article. Remember that only rarely should you quote another author's work. Magazines compete with each other, they don't give credit to each other. That's the key difference between writing for publication and writing for a grade in an English composition class.

Observation—This certainly is one of the most nonthreatening kinds of research to conduct, since it merely involves watching and taking notes. For example, if you are writing a profile of a well-known person, you might arrange to follow him around for a day, both on the job and at home. Notice how he interacts with his family and colleagues (and how they respond to him); observe his body language, his choices of food and music, his style of clothing, his favorite expressions and, of course, his physical appearance.

Participation—Here the writer jumps in and involves himself in his article. Writing about hot-air ballooning? Arrange to go for an early-morning drift over the countryside. Assigned to do a feature on a college basketball star? Slip into your Nikes and go one-on-one with him on a basketball court. But be careful: The temptation is to write first-person accounts of your experiences, and this shifts the emphasis away from the topic and toward the writer. Many editors veto all articles that smack of "I-strain." Unless you are a celebrity, such as George Plimpton, never cast yourself in the role of the star.

Interviews—The key to many writing projects is interviewing, an activity that only *looks* so easy. Oprah, for example, well-prepared with her list of probing questions, coaxes insightful comments from a famous guest during a cozy tête-à-tête, as millions of viewers "eavesdrop" from home. This glamorous scenario, in the eyes of many beginning writers, constitutes a typical interview.

But there's nothing typical about it.

Interviews are at the heart of almost every piece of nonfiction writing. Rarely does a week go by that a working writer doesn't conduct an interview or two or three; yet only a small portion of these are one-on-ones with celebrities. To illustrate the point, let's revisit the writing projects discussed previously.

• Remember the writer who was assigned to write about the phenomenon of doll collecting in America? She began her research at the library, progressed to toy shops and doll shows, and culminated with interviews with doll makers, designers, collectors, antique dealers, and retailers. The library, toy shop, and doll show prepared her well for the interview phase. By the time she sat down to talk with the experts, she knew enough about the topic to ask thoughtful questions.

• And the author who trekked the streets of Detroit for an upcoming book not only visited key landmarks, but he also interviewed people who lived and worked in the area. Their guidance helped him understand and appreciate life in an industrial mecca of the Midwest.

• When the travel writer wrote her feature about the Lillehammer Olympics, she accompanied it with a sidebar based on a telephone interview with Norwegian runner Grete Waitz, eight-time winner of the New York Marathon and an Olympic silver medalist. As Norway's most famous female athlete, Waitz talked about her country's long sports tradition and their efforts to launch a national fitness program in connection with the Games.

These three examples illustrate the textbook definition of an interview— "communication with a purpose." You, the interviewer, are asking questions and gathering information for the specific purpose of using it in a piece of your writing. The interview can be as informal as a quick phone call to ask an opinion or verify a fact, or it can be as formal as a lengthy, face-to-face taping session.

The four interview-related questions that free lancers most frequently ask are:

• How do we select the sources we should interview for an article?

• How do we convince a person that he or she should grant us an interview (especially if we are new to this writing business and haven't established our credibility)?

• Where can we find national sources, apart from people in our home town?

• How do we conduct a professional interview?

Let's answer each of these questions, beginning with the dilemma of choosing the best persons to interview for a writing project.

Selecting experts

How you select your interviewees depends upon what you are writing and what kind of specific information you need. If you are working on an article about World War II concentration camps, you would try to interview someone who had been a prisoner in one of these camps. Additionally, you would talk to a professor of World War II history; a staff member at the Holocaust Museum in Washington, D.C.; and a psychologist who can discuss the long-term impact of a concentration-camp experience.

If your nonfiction project involves pulling together comments and opinions from a variety of sources, you may conduct several brief telephone interviews and use only two or three quotations gleaned from each call. The challenge here is to talk with people who have different points of view and represent different geographic locations, ages, and backgrounds. An award-winning journalist who wrote a magazine article on female members of Generation X interviewed college students, young wives, and working women from several states. The interviews ranged from a few minutes to an hour, yet each source accounted for only a small part of the final manuscript.

Usually the most in-depth interviews are reserved for profile articles. In these, the interviewee is the main focus, and she or he will be quoted, observed, and described. Seasoned profile writers also conduct secondary interviews with people who know the primary interviewee and will present other views—positive and negative—of the profiled personality. (For practice, do the exercise on the facing page.)

Every direct quotation you include in an article must be accompanied by an attribution explaining who the speaker is. Since it is through attributions that you establish the credibility of your sources, you should try to schedule interviews with people whose titles command authority (chairman of the board, chief of staff, president and CEO, or director of a program, for example). An executive vice president of a bank is going to have more credibility than a teller; a full professor is going to have more authority than a first-year instructor; the police chief is going to have more impact than a third-shift patrolman.

How to convince experts to grant interviews

Many beginning free lancers fear that they will be unable to schedule interviews with quotable sources because they are not well-known writers and have few, if any, published credits.

This is less of a problem than it seems. Many sources—particularly academics who have spent their lives researching and studying a subject—are flattered to be asked to discuss their areas of expertise. A good query letter can provide the leverage necessary to convince other, less enthusiastic people to give up some of their valuable time. There are three points at which you can send a query to an editor:

• After you've developed an idea for an article or book but you haven't conducted any research

The Questions

Assignment: Choose a person you would like to interview (living, dead, famous, infamous). Assume that you have thirty minutes of this person's time. Devise a list of ten questions you would ask him/her. Remember to phrase your questions so they will elicit as much information as possible. Arrange your questions in logical order: Save your toughest questions for last; ask questions that show you have done your homework and know something about your interviewee.

The person I want to interview is _____.

The purpose of my article is _____.

The questions I would ask are:

1.

2.

3.

4.

5.

6.

7.

8.

9.

10.

Note: Every article—even a profile—should contain comments from at least two people. After you have completed the exercise above, decide who your second interview would be to add perspective to your first interview. What would you ask the second person?

- After you've gathered all your research (library, observations, participation, interviews)
- After you've written your article or book

The first way is preferable. By sending a query early in the idea stage you can see if an editor is interested in your proposal *before* you invest time and money in it. Also, if your idea is a good one and the editor replies that he or she would like to see the finished manuscript on speculation, you then can approach the sources whom you want to interview and say that Jane Smith, editor of such-and-such magazine, has asked to see the article. This gives your prospective interviewee the assurance that his time will be well spent because publication is a real possibility.

In your attempt to convince credible sources to talk with you, never make the mistake of offering payment for an interview; submitting your list of questions to the interviewee in advance of the interview; or agreeing to let the interviewee read the article before you submit it to the editor. Instead, ask permission to tape record the session to ensure accuracy. Paying for an interview creates an impression that since the interviewee is getting paid, he should say what you want him to say. Submitting questions in advance robs your interview of spontaneity and allows your source to create, with the help of others, "responses by committee." Allowing your source to approve your final draft opens you up to demands for revisions that differ from what he actually said and can sap your manuscript of your style and insights.

Finding national sources

If you live in Des Moines, Iowa, but you hope to sell an article to a magazine that boasts a national circulation, your interviewees can't all live in Greater Des Moines. Locating national sources is not the problem it once was, thanks to communication technology. Listed below are seven ways— some traditional and some cutting edge—that you can gain access to credible, quotable sources.

- *Public relations representatives.* Every hospital, college, industry, governmental agency, politician, church denominiation, city, and sports team or event has a publicist or public relations (PR) expert whose responsibilities include accommodating interview requests from writers. A good PR person can provide a writer with background information, photos, interviews, and tours of facilities. All the writer has to do is ask.
- *Other authors.* As you do your library research, take note of any researcher who has written about some facet of your topic. If he is a book author, you can contact him through his publishing house. If he writes for a magazine, write to him in care of the publication, even though he may not be on staff. The editors will forward your correspondence to him.
- *Celebrities.* Be aware in advance of any well-known personality who is

planning to visit your city. Then query a magazine and propose an interview with the celebrity. If the editor suggests that you pursue the subject, get in touch with the organization sponsoring the celebrity's visit. If the sponsor isn't authorized to set up interviews, ask for the name of the celebrity's publicist. With the assurance that a specific editor at a specific magazine is interested in a piece about him or her, the publicist is likely to set up an interview. But all this takes time, so begin the process early.

• *ProfNet.* Linked by the Internet, this is a cooperative of public information officers (PIOs) who provide journalists and authors convenient access to expert sources. It is coordinated by the Office of University Affairs at the State University of New York at Stony Brook. The procedure is easy: A writer submits a brief explanation of her writing project and where it will be published. Then she specifies the kind of expertise she needs. The request is delivered electronically into the e-mail boxes of PIOs at about 600 colleges, universities, and a range of government, corporate, and nonprofit entities in 16 countries. PIOs respond by sending names and telephone numbers of expert sources from their institutions who are willing to speak on the topic the writer is researching. The writer follows up with telephone interviews.

• *College, university, and seminary rosters.* Even if you are not into electronic communication, you can certainly tap the expertise that is available at U.S. universities and colleges, many of which today publish "expert guides" that list names and brief biographies of faculty members. For example, the Southwestern University School of Law in Los Angeles prints a 68-page guide that details more than 120 legal issues and topics that its faculty members are qualified to discuss with writers. Timely issues include: parental rights, palimony, politically correct speech, sexual harassment, gay and lesbian issues, battered person syndrome defense, and living wills.

• *Electronic bulletin boards and interactive information services.* If you have a computer, telephone, and a modem, you can collect comments and interview sources from around the world without leaving your home. For example, a huge information service such as CompuServe (based in Columbus, Ohio) has dozens of special interest groups (called forums) that meet online. If you are doing an article about gardening, you can log onto the gardening forum, post a message or question on the electronic bulletin board, and log off. Check your electronic mailbox a few hours later and you most likely will find a variety of responses waiting for you. These replies come from users around the world and can be followed up with phone interviews or on-line question-and-answer exchanges.

• *Collect business cards.* Any time you attend a professional meeting, convention, writers' workshop, or any other mass gathering, offer to trade business cards with as many participants as you can. Write reminder notes to yourself on the backs of the cards. ("Dr. Brown is an expert in Attention

Deficit Disorder"; "Eleanor Jones has home-schooled five children"; "Robert Elliott builds solar homes.") Try to collect cards from persons who live in other states and represent various interests.

Tips on conducting interviews

On the facing page is a checklist that will help you conduct your interviews. Several tips need to be underscored. For example, the interview process actually begins when you place the telephone call requesting the interview. It is essential that you establish control the moment you make contact. Explain your project, the reason you want to set up an appointment, how much time you need, and where you propose to conduct the meeting. If you create a friendly but professional impression, your potential source is very likely to agree to the interview.

Ideally, an interview is conducted at the person's home or office, where he will be relaxed and you can get a sense of his personal environment. The most unfavorable timing and place are at noon in a restaurant, or at the end of the day when the subject is anxious to go home, or right before he is due at a meeting.

The order in which you ask your questions and the way you phrase them will often determine the success of an interview. Save the toughest questions for the end, and never ask a question that can be answered "yes" or "no." Prepare more questions than you think you will need, begin with a challenging but not unfriendly question, and strive to elicit the person's thoughts rather than a litany of facts that are available elsewhere. No matter how experienced you are as an interviewer, always prepare yourself with a written list of questions arranged in some logical order. The list serves as a blueprint for the interview and helps keep you from wandering from your topic.

Always record interviews on tape. This assures accuracy, allows you to sit back and maintain eye contact, and helps improve your interview skills. When you play back the tape, critique your performance as an interviewer. Did you allow the source to tug you off course? Did you ask good follow-up questions? Did you avoid important questions because they might be "uncomfortable"? Did you ask permission to do a subsequent phone interview if you found that you needed additional information?

A good source may be interviewed numerous times in the course of a writer's career. The smart author keeps a little black book full of experts' names and telephone numbers. To make sure that a valuable source will agree to future interviews, a writer should follow a few rules of etiquette: Be prepared for your interview (a lack of preparation sends the message that you don't think the source is very important); be professional during your meeting (you are there to gather information, not make a new friend); as you write your article, double-check any data that you find confusing;

Interview Tips

- When setting up an interview, tell your subject what you want to discuss.
- Set the parameters on how much time you need.
- Never overstay the amount of time you requested.
- Read everything available on the interviewee.
- Prepare a list of questions in logical order.
- Try to conduct the interview on the interviewee's home turf.
- Avoid meeting in noisy, public places.
- Save the toughest questions for last.
- Observe your interviewee's body language.
- Strive for thoughts, opinions, feelings.
- Plan to spend most of your time listening.
- Be tough, not cruel.
- Use a tape recorder, but also take notes.
- Don't interrupt answers.
- Try not to have other persons present.
- Don't try to find out everything about a subject; focus on one or two areas.
- Don't worry about lulls—give your subject time to reflect.
- Get a second opinion—schedule secondary interviews with associates.
- Don't wait too long to write up the interview.
- Leave yourself out of the final manuscript (no first person!).
- Follow up with a thank-you note and a tear sheet.

send a short thank-you note immediately after the interview; and send a tear sheet of the published article as soon as it appears in print.

Techniques of Outlining

Be honest. At some point during your student days you were undoubtedly assigned a research paper with the stipulaton that you submit an outline with it. Convinced that outlines are exercises to please teachers or professors rather than tools to help writers, you dutifully wrote your paper and *then* concocted an outline from it. And what a piece of work it was: snappy Roman numerals, thoughtful topic sentences, supporting information arranged in proper A-B-C order, and minor details listed in 1-2-3 format.

Many professional writers are guilty of the same offense. Not until you begin to write for publication will you fully appreciate the value of creating outlines for most of your writing projects. In fact, some writers often create *two* outlines for each article that they tackle. The preliminary version is like a scribbled game plan. They jot down their idea, the purpose of the piece, the major points they plan to cover, and the type of research required to produce a salable article or book. This informal exercise bears little resemblance to the outlines required in composition class. It boasts no Roman numerals, topic sentences, A-B-Cs or 1-2-3s. It functions more as a to-do list that moves an idea out of incubation and onto paper. Not until you quickly work your way through the outline will you know if you have a viable project that you will want to pursue. Only then should you decide if you will want to visit the library and begin the serious business of collecting material, scheduling interviews, and writing query letters.

Create your second outline *after* you have done most of your research. At this point, an outline with help you in these eight ways:

• *It will tell you whether you have the makings of a book or an article.* A lot of book proposals describe ideas that would make dynamite articles, but the content simply isn't strong enough to sustain a 200-page book. The author who prepares a chapter-by-chapter outline knows what he has—and what he doesn't have—before he approaches an editor.

• *It will give you focus.* When we began on our book *How to Stop Living for the Applause,* our plan was to probe the topic of workaholism among women. But after we assembled our research and began to fashion an outline, we saw the need to refine the subject further. The word "workaholism" has become a dumping ground for such diverse conditions as perfectionism, driven behavior, high achievement, and overachievement. Harnessed, workaholism can be a healthy and productive condition. Unchecked, it can be a symptom of serious emotional problems. We decided to focus our book on perfectionism and gear it to female readers who recognize their perfectionist tendencies and want to learn self-help techniques to control them.

- *It will help you pace your project.* Think of a book or an article as a journey that is traversed in measured steps from a starting point to a finish line. By looking at your outline you can tell if you're moving in the right direction, if you're likely to stall in the middle, if your "traveling" will be done in fits and starts, and if the overall content will carry you to a strong conclusion. (How many times have you started a book, loved the first 25 pages, then lost interest as the text took confusing detours or ran out of momentum?)

- *It will break a book project into pieces.* Don't let yourself be intimidated by the idea that you have to produce a 220-page manuscript by a certain date. If you have been writing articles for years, keep in mind that a book is very much like a collection of articles joined by a common thread. Rather than worrying about creating 220 pages, concern yourself with writing an opening segment of 20 pages, no more and no less. A good outline will help you break down your book-length project into bite-sized segments of related material. Chapter headings will evolve after you group major points, supporting anecdotes, facts, and illustrations.

- *It will help you diagnose thin areas.* As you sort the research material you've gathered and put it under chapter labels, you'll begin to see areas that are weak or repetitive. You then have two options: Either consolidate chapters or search for additional material to strengthen the weak ones. This same exercise will show you which chapters have too much content, in which case you can divide the overburdened chapter into two or more chapters, or you can distribute the extra material among all chapters.

- *An outline helps you see how the book or article should be organized.* A strong outline will show a natural and logical flow from one point to the next. Often chronological order is not the best way to organize a piece of writing. For example, a book about the true case of the tracking down and capture of a serial killer may begin dramatically by describing the scene of one of the murders and then flashing back to the days in which the killer stalked his intended victim. An outline will help the writer plan flashbacks that will not distract from the main story.

- *It points out natural breaks.* Chapters in a book should begin with a bang to engage the reader at once; they also need to end with a bang to convince the reader to keep turning the pages. An outline will help you see where one segment should end and another begin.

- *It allows you to control the length of the manuscript.* Most editors and publishers have a preferred word or page count. If a writer merely feeds a roll of paper into her printer and begins tapping at the keyboard without a blueprint of the finished product, she can become entrenched in detail and be at the 500-page mark before covering half the material in the book. Few publishers today are interested in a 1,000-page manuscript, so the writer faces the huge task of pruning words, slashing paragraphs, and cutting her work by half. On the other hand, if a writer has outlined a book of 12 chapters and has decided that each chapter will contain 20 pages, he or she knows at the outset that the final draft will be about 240 pages.

What kind of outline is best? Use the one that works for you. Some writers like to record their research on 3" x 5" index cards. This system allows them to create stacks—one stack of cards per chapter if they are working on a book, or one stack per major point if they are working on an article. They arrange the cards within each stack in a logical order. As they add research, they rearrange the stack to include the additions. If one stack becomes too thick, it can be divided into two. When the number of stacks and the order of the cards seems right, the cards can be taped together into an arrangement that resembles an accordion.

Other writers use a variation of the mind-mapping exercise (see Phase Four of this book). Use a sheet of paper to represent either a major point of an article or a chapter of a book. The central idea is contained in a circle in the center of the page. Offshoot ideas (subpoints) spring from the central idea. Support material is connected to each idea.

Whenever you are working on an article assignment, you might want to try using color-coded highlighter pens. First, make a fat file of research material (interviews, notes, statistics, background articles from the library). You probably will have accumulated much more information than can be included in one article. Second, choose a slant for the article and come up with a creative title and coverline that capture the slant. Finally, read through every piece of research that you've assembled in your file, referring frequently to your slant to make sure you don't stray from your chosen focus. Whenever you come across any piece of research material that relates to your coverline, highlight it with a single color highlighter pen. When you spot a possible lead or a possible ending for your article, scribble a question mark in the margin.

An informal outline emerges from this exercise. Mentally, you'll disregard all material that isn't highlighted. Review possible leads and endings and select your favorites. Then arrange the highlighted material in a logical order. This gives you the structure of your article. After you've written and submitted your manuscript, duplicate the exercise. Select a second coverline and use a different colored pen to highlight material that supports the new coverline. In this way, you can create other articles from the same file of information.

Creating Winning Titles

Coming up with a great title for a book, chapter, or article is not easy, but it is less of a chore if you learn some simple brainstorming techniques.

Few best-selling books are burdened with extremely long titles—yes, David Reuben's *Everything You Always Wanted to Know About Sex (But Were Afraid to Ask)* is an important exception! A good title is usually brief, often catchy, always clear, to-the-point, and has punch. The "punch" part is more easily explained by example rather than definition: *Future Shock* was a far more effective title for Alvin Toffler's bestseller than *The Future of Our World* would have been.

Sometimes, a good title is as simple as one well-chosen word: *Alive* by Piers Paul Read, *UnRetirement* by Catherine D. Fyock and Anne Marrs Dorton, *Iacocca* by Lee Iacocca with William Novak, and *Wishcraft* by Barbara Sher.

Test your title on people. If heads turn and eyes light up, you may have a winner. If only a "polite" response is generated, keep trying to come up with something better. Titles are little billboards; they are meant to "sell" your manuscript. Remember that because titles are sales tools, the names you propose for your manuscripts may not be the titles that eventually emerge in print. Magazine editors routinely rewrite titles of articles to capture reader interest and to fit the style of the publication and its specialized readership. For example, some publications always use a short "label" title and follow it with a more descriptive subhead. Together, the two elements—the head and subhead—offer the reader a clear idea of the article's content:

Good Grief
Do recovery groups help or hinder healing?

The title works well because it combines a short, familiar phrase (Good Grief) with a question that both explains the content and challenges the reader to jump in and guess at the answer. Other publications, including newspapers, may prefer simple declarative headlines:

Therapists Argue Value of Recovery Groups

The smart free lancer studies a periodical, picks up on its title/headline format, and gives his manuscript a name that fits in perfectly with the magazine's established style.

Choosing the right title for a book is even more important than selecting article titles. Books are more permanent and costly than magazines, and the right name can enhance or diminish the chances of success. Small wonder that a title is such an important decision that a publishing house often involves its marketing staff in the deliberations. Unless the author has retained the right to approve or reject a title, he may have to accept whatever choice the publisher makes. The author would do well to remember that the publishing company is just as anxious as he is for the book to succeed; therefore, any final decisions related to the marketplace should be made with input from the marketing experts. In short, an author should aggressively build a case for the title he prefers; but, if overruled, he should accept the group's verdict and hope he never has to say, "I told you so."

Every manuscript you submit to a publisher should have a working title even if the marketing gurus are likely to veto it. A title gives a manuscript an identity as the manuscript is passed around and discussed among editors. Here are five short questions to ask yourself as you attempt to create a strong working title:

• *Is it a cliché?* If so, change it. Readers yawn over shopworn expressions such as *A Penny Saved Is a Penny Earned* (finance book) or *Off the Beaten Track* (travel guidebook). Be original.

• *Is it bland?* Nobody wants to read something called *Life in Smithville.* Give it some pizzazz.

• *Does it clearly relate to your topic?* Use the specific title *Tips on Flying Biplanes* rather than the ambiguous title *Up in the Clouds.*

• *Can it be pronounced without difficulty?* Remember that word of mouth sells most books, so don't give your book a title that contains a foreign phrase or unknown word that people find hard to repeat or remember.

• *Does it reveal too much?* Don't call your true-life detective book *The Twin Brother Was the Killer.*

If you feel that developing a good title for your manuscript may be difficult for you, apply the techniques explained in the "Creating Great Titles" exercise on the facing page. You may have to work your way through the entire process before you come up with the perfect name, but the effort will be worth it. Once you hear it, you'll say, "That's it!"

Creating Coverlines

Have you ever bought an issue of a magazine because you were attracted by the promising or provocative words arranged on the publication's cover? If so, you're not alone. Coverlines—the essence of articles, distilled to about five words and placed on the front of a magazine—are the reason many magazine buyers select one publication over another on a newsstand. The decision often is unconscious and is made within seconds. The reader believes that by buying the periodical she will discover the solution to a problem, the answer to a question, or will finally have the precise information she needs to improve her life in some way.

A free-lance writer who can capture the essence of an article in a catchy phrase has a better chance of selling it than the writer who merely proposes an idea or offers a title. Make no mistake, coverlines are the responsibility of editors. However, a writer who thinks in terms of coverlines, understands their importance, and includes them in query letters is much valued. For example, in approaching an editor about an article commemorating the 25th anniversary of Weight Watchers International, don't begin your query

Creating Great Titles:
A Brainstorming Exercise

It may take a lot of brainstorming to come up with a perfect title for your manuscript, but the process can be simplified if you try to adapt the subject of your material to the following 16 types of titles. Keeping one of your manuscripts in mind, come up with a title for it in each of the following categories.

1. The Reversal Title
    Example: *One Bad Deed Deserves Another*

2. The Challenge Title
    Example: *Can You Improve Your Health Insurance?*

3. The Terse Summary Title
    Example: *Hinckley Shoots Reagan*

4. The Superlative Title
    Example: *The Most Expensive Weekend Vacation*

5. The Numerical Title
    Example: *Five Ways to Improve Family Communication*

6. The Negative Title
    Example: *No Schooling, No Job, No Future*

7. The Ironic Title
    Example: *Night Watchmen More Useful During Day*

8. The Paradox Title
    Example: *I'll Always Love the Man I Hate*

9. The Blunt Statement Title
    Example: *Don't Say It with Flowers!*

10. The Comedy Title
    Example: *Hoo Sez Eye Kan't Spel Korectly?*

11. The Inside Scoop Title
    Example: *What Single Women Will Do to Get Married*

12. The Contrast Title
    Example: *The Youngest Champ, the Youngest Has-Been*

13. The Alliteration Title
    Example: *Tight Turns Taunt Truckers*

14. The Rhyming Title
    Example: *Dress for Success*

15. The Pun Title
    Example: *A Thyme for All Seasonings*

16. The Teaching Title
    Example: *How to Be a Better Time Manager*

letter with the mundane sentence: "Next year, Weight Watchers will mark its silver anniversary. . . ." Instead, start with a three-word paragraph that an editor will recognize as an eye-catching coverline: *Hip, Hips Away!*

Coverlines should be similar to the title of an article so the reader who bought the magazine because of its catchy coverlines can easily find the articles referred to. Because of their brevity, however, coverlines often must be expanded by a few words to make descriptive titles. *Hip, Hips Away!* works well as a coverline; *At 25, Weight Watchers Still Cheer "Hip, Hips Away!"* is an effective title.

Creating coverlines is a skill that becomes easier with practice. Here are several strategies that editors use as they try to compress whole articles to irresistible phrases:

● Promise the reader something: *New Cure For Depression; Flying High at Low Cost; How to Recharge Low-Voltage Relationships.*

● Make the reader smile: *Irish Drives Beguiling; Grecian Formula—One Part Sun, One Part Sea; Doggone Vet Costs.*

● Ask readers a question: *Will In-Car Computers Replace Road Maps? Prayer or Prozac?*

If you have trouble capturing your article in a clever phrase, your topic may lack focus or, worse yet, be boring. Work through the "Winners and Losers" exercise on the facing page to help you identify article ideas that you should pursue and those you should discard.

As you become acquainted with the coverline concept, remember that the success of some periodicals—in-flight magazines, trade journals and membership publications—is not affected by the words on their covers. They have built-in readerships, and their editors don't have to worry about circulation being "up" or "down" from issue to issue. Such magazines aren't available on newsstands and don't depend on single-copy sales for their revenue. If you fly TWA, you are offered a complimentary copy of *TWA Ambassador* when you board; if you belong to the Public Relations Society of America, you receive *Public Relations Journal* every month; if you are a member of Phi Delta Kappa education fraternity, you are sent *The Kappan*. Often these magazines view coverlines as distracting and prefer to limit the elements on their cover to a strong photo or illustration and the publication's logo.

Leads: Off to the Right Start

Your parents and your teachers were forever telling you as a child that "well begun is half done." In writing, that may not be literally true, but often it feels that way. Once a writer gets over the initial hump of coming up with a great lead, the rest of the article often seems as easy as a downhill glide.

Winners and Losers

How do you know if an article idea is marketable and should be offered to an editor via a query? Try this test: Distill your idea to a coverline. Next to the coverline, describe the content of your article in one or two sentences. Ask yourself: Is this idea timely? Does it appeal to a wide range of readers? Is it fresh? Can I cover it in 2,000 words? As practice, evaluate each of the article ideas below. Eliminate "losers" and rank the "winners" by salability.

Coverline	Explanation of content
_____ School Daze	Why I home-schooled my son
_____ Feelin' Your Oats	How oat bran can lower cholesterol
_____ The 3 Best Country Inns of the South	Where iced tea is served by a butler named Rhett
_____ Ladies of the House	Mini profiles of five Congresswomen
_____ It's 10 p.m., Do You Know Where _Your_ Mother Is?	How to handle a widowed mom's decision to date, remarry
_____ Kept Women	Wives who choose home over careers
_____ Joys of Christmas Past	Retirees recall best holiday memories

Possible answers: We'd eliminate _School Daze, Feelin' Your Oats, Kept Women,_ and _Joys of Christmas Past. School Daze_ might be salvaged if it is expanded beyond one woman's story and includes views of parents, educators, and home-schooled youth who are now adults. Still, the story has been done too often. _Feelin' Your Oats_ is a cliché as a coverline and a bore as a topic. Another tired topic is _Kept Women—_ a coverline guaranteed to alienate everyone. _Joys of Christmas Past_ may be suitable for a local newspaper but would be of little interest to editors of national publications. _The 3 Best Inns_ could work for a travel section of a newspaper or magazine because it is tightly focused and promises to share a secret with readers. _Ladies of the House_ isn't a new idea but it has the advantage of offering not one but five success stories. _It's 10 p.m., Do You Know Where_ Your _Mother Is?_ is a timely topic if geared to middle-aged readers who face the common problem that "mom" isn't acting her age.

Rather than jumping right into writing the lead, it is best to take a few minutes to think through what you are about to write. What sort of readers will be reading this article? Will they be children or adolescents or adults? If it is an informative piece, will it be read by laypeople or professionals? Answering these questions will determine what level of vocabulary you will use and whether or not you can use technical terms.

Next, what is your purpose in writing this piece? Do you want to teach, entertain, analyze, critique, report, describe, record, or do all of these? Every article has a purpose. Some have two or three: a primary purpose and one or two secondary purposes. (Just because you are reporting on something doesn't mean you can't be entertaining at the same time.) Determining your purpose will help you decide whether to use anecdotes, facts, opinions, research and/or quotations in your feature. The "What's Your Purpose?" exercise on the facing page will help you establish an intent for your manuscript.

Having thought through your objectives, you now need to write a lead that will excite the reader. You are trying to tease or induce the reader to venture into the body of the article. Let's examine a few of the most commonly (and successfully) used leads:

The *shocking statement* lead presents a statement that jolts readers, compelling them to continue to read. For example, if you were going to do a feature about a Hollywood make-up artist, you might begin with, "How would you like to look twenty years younger in three hours?" The reader would want to read a few more lines to see how such an occurrence could be possible.

The *direct statement* is the sort of lead that calls out to the reader, in effect saying, "Hey, you! Pay attention! What I am about to say has a direct bearing on your life. Yes, *you!*" For example, if you were writing an article about seeing a doctor for a cholesterol test, your lead might be, "A three-minute test may add 10 years to your life." The reader wonders, "I could live an extra 10 years? How?" To find out, he will have to keep reading. You will have hooked him.

The *descriptive lead* works well to establish the dramatic setting of an article. If you were going to write about how Hurricane Andrew hit Miami, you might begin by describing the tomb-like silence that enveloped the city in the minutes just before the hurricane hit. ("No birds were chirping, no televisions were playing, no people were talking, no cars were moving on the streets. Everyone was just *waiting* for it.") Then, in contrast, you could describe the cacophonous blast of the oncoming storm. ("Sirens were blaring, babies were screaming, plate glass windows were shattering, trees were snapping in half.") The extreme differences in description would put the reader in the midst of the chaos.

The *quotation lead* can be used in several ways. If your feature is about a

What's Your Purpose?

Every article, every short story, every book has a purpose. Sometimes the purpose of a manuscript is as simple as "to entertain" or as ambitious as "to decipher." Ask yourself these two questions: *What's my purpose? What reaction do I hope to elicit from my readers?* Specifically, do you want to make readers laugh? Cry? Do you want to teach them how to do something? Inform them of something they may not know? Influence them to think a certain way? An effective piece of writing leaves readers slightly changed for having read the piece—wiser, happier, motivated, inspired, persuaded. The talented writer knows the response he wants before he writes his opening paragraph.

Before launching your next writing project, review the list of verbs below. Choose your purpose; know the response you want. Tip: It's very likely you will have more than one purpose for every piece of writing you do. For example, you may want to inform *and* entertain your reader.

Advise	Help	Prepare
Advocate	Honor	Prevent
Amuse	Illustrate	Recruit
Analyze	Influence	Report
Announce	Inform	Simplify
Clarify	Inspire	Stimulate
Condense	Interpret	Suggest
Debunk	Motivate	Support
Describe	Notify	Teach
Entertain	Presuade	Titillate
Evaluate	Probe	Uplift
Explain	Propose	Vindicate

Assignment: Read an article in a general-interest magazine and try to determine the writer's primary purpose and secondary purpose(s).

celebrity, you may open with a direct quotation from that person, i.e., "I am a very good housekeeper," says Zsa Zsa Gabor. "Each time I get a divorce, I keep the house." A variation is to use a pithy or humorous quotation that is not immediately recognizable, yet is perfect for beginning a discussion of your topic. The sources for such quotations must be cited. For example, an article about the increasing number of women executives in corporate America started with, "Ah, the woman: Why can't she be more like the man?" and then cited the source as Prof. Henry Higgins in *My Fair Lady*. A third variation involves taking a familiar quotation and giving it a surprise ending. For example, you might write, "You can't make an omelette without breaking some eggheads," for an article about scientists who are puzzling over how to breed chickens that will lay double-yolked eggs.

The *pun lead* can be fun if you remember a fine line separates a clever play on words from something that is just silly. Make sure your pun is easy to understand and truly applies to your topic. For example, a pun lead for an article on reforestation might begin, "Pine growers' thumbs are ever green." A pun lead for a cooking article might begin, "A thyme has come for all seasonings."

The *summary lead* uses as much Who, What, When, Where, Why, and How material as possible. What it lacks in creativity it makes up for in information. Newspapers love summary leads, as do magazines. For example, a summary lead about an unusual wedding couple might begin, "Mary Brown has spent her life in a wheelchair since she was struck down by a truck operated by a drunken driver on New Year's Eve in 1975. This Saturday she will 'walk' down the aisle and marry her doctor."

The *anecdotal lead* provides a little story or a short account of an interesting (and often amusing) incident relative to the subject of the article. It can be as short as one or two sentences, or as long as a couple of paragraphs. It can be a story about you or about someone you know or have read about that serves as an illustration or an example of what you plan to discuss. For that reason, it works well as an introduction. A split anecdote—the first half at the beginning of the article and the rest at the end, serving as a wrap-up—can also work well.

The *combination lead* incorporates two or more of the leads just discussed. For example, the following lead contains a shocking statement, a quotation, and a description: "The Yukon was heartless," Sgt. Decker said, pointing to the nub of his arm. "When I lost my glove, I lost my hand."

The best way to discover other kinds of leads is to skim interviews, essays, and articles and make a list of the various ways writers begin their works. Some will use breakneck-action scenes (a car chase, a gun fight, a storm at sea); others will use intriguing dialogue (a cross examination, a cry for help, a startling question, words of sympathy) or comedy (a joke or pun); and still others will use an element of suspense (by letting the reader know of impending danger which the subject in the article is not yet aware of).

No matter which type of lead is used, the key point is to grab the reader's attention and hold it. If you can hook readers from line one to line two, you can probably get them to move to paragraph two, and then to column two, and then to page two . . . and then, suddenly, the article will end and the reader will be amazed at how quickly it progressed.

Mastering Effective Endings

Many writers focus all their efforts on developing a good lead, reasoning that if they can't hook the reader at the beginning there isn't any need to worry about the end. But that's false logic. For sustained careers in nonfiction writing, writers must be as adept at closings as they are at leads, whether it is a one-paragraph conclusion to an article or the final chapter of a long book.

Endings should have an impact on readers, should make them feel the article has followed a logical course of events and arrived purposely and correctly at a specific place.

There are five common problem endings writers should avoid:

● The *unresolved ending* leaves readers wondering exactly how the events in the piece turned out. Readers like to know the way things were resolved or at least to feel pretty sure of what will happen.

● The *redundant ending* that rehashes everything that has already been said in the article is tedious. If material has been presented in a logical, intriguing way, recap is unnecessary, unless the topic is so complicated that the writer wants to emphasize a few key points at the end.

● The *listless ending* just loses steam until it comes to a slow stop. Once the required word count has been reached, the writer quits, and readers are left with a ho-hum opinion of the piece.

● The *prejudiced ending* tries to tell the reader what conclusions to draw from the material and what action to take. Readers want to be presented with well-researched, unbiased facts so that they can make up their own minds about matters. They do not want a writer telling them, "So, as you can plainly see, the Republican Party has the only platform worth considering this November." The readers will decide for themselves.

● The *unrelated ending* diverges from the main subject of the piece. For example, an article about boating through the Everglades should not shift to a discussion of rowboats and end with a comment on how to select one that is seaworthy.

To avoid creating one of these weak closings, keep a sheet marked "Endings" in your research file or notebook. As you conduct interviews and dig out background material for your next article, write down any powerful one-liners, amazing facts, or captivating anecdotes that you feel might make good endings. Also, try the endings exercise on the facing page.

Creating an ending that has style and impact takes effort. Most experienced writers know their endings before they write their leads. Otherwise, it's like a traveler beginning a trip with no destination in mind.

Breaking Through Writer's Block

Writer's block—the inability to come up with creative ideas—is often brought on by physical exhaustion, tedium, loss of confidence, or a lack of proper incentives.

It isn't enough to say to a writer in these circumstances, "Get some rest, start believing in yourself, and meet that deadline." Writers don't respond to platitudes. They need processes and procedures to follow.

And a system that works for one writer may not necessarily work for another. The prolific Isaac Asimov used to sit amidst four typewriters, each with a different writing assignment. If he hit a snag on one, he'd simply swivel his chair and work on another. "When I get back to the problem, my unconscious has solved it," he explained. Another successful writer says he likes to dress for work and then go to the office . . . even though "the office" is just down the hall from his bedroom. By thinking of his writing as a business, he works in a more businesslike manner.

Beating writer's block is often a psychological trick. Still, if it works, that's all that counts. It is important for writers not to deceive themselves into thinking they are being productive when they are only filling time with activities.

Anything that draws you away from writing is downtime. You cannot justify reading novels, attending movies, browsing through the library, interviewing interesting people, watching television, talking on the phone, or listening to entertaining tapes as ways of beating writer's block. These are all fine writing-related activities, but they should be pursued *after* your day's writing is done, not *instead* of the writing.

Here are some tips on breaking writer's block:

• *Keep writing anyway.* Do a "free write." Just put down anything that comes to your mind. After you fill up several pages, you can go back and edit the grammar, punctuation, syntax, and spelling. Or, try revising something you wrote earlier, just to get back on track. (See page 41.)

• *Alter viewpoints.* If you cannot think of how to explain something in more detail from one point of view, turn to another. You've explained how the police view car jackings; try to write down how the criminals view them. If you've explained the anxiety a person feels when applying for a new job,

How to Develop Effective Endings

Listed below are five techniques you can experiment with in learning how to write effective endings for your articles and chapters. Take something you are now working on and try to use each of these procedures to write a closing for your manuscript. Which one works best? Why?

The Echo Effect—If your lead presents a problem, let your ending present an answer. If your lead asks a riddle, have your ending provide the solution. If your lead calls out a challenge, let your closing echo a response. In this way, your lead and your closing will serve as bookends for your piece.

The Ironic Twist—Offer an unexpected yet logical ending to your article. You might profile a man who has spent twenty years in prison breaking rocks; when he is released, the only job he is able to find is at a gravel company ... breaking rocks.

The Powerful Quotation—A quotation from someone featured in your article can provide a dramatic summary. Example: "Most preachers give you sermons that tell you, 'You can't take it with you,'" said the government agent in Guyana, "but the Rev. Jim Jones seems to have had a different idea.'"

The Joke or Pun— The vaudeville adage of "Leave 'em laughin'" has validity for an article. A bit of lightheartedness leaves a reader smiling. Appropriate ad libs, puns, jokes, or humorous anecdotes can both summarize an article and also provide entertainment.

The Amen Affirmation—An ending that presents irrefutable facts can affirm the situation and allow the reader to nod understandably. Example: "The enemy interrogators had taken away Captain Wilson's freedom, his clothes, his food, and his proximity to other soldiers. The thing they were never able to take away from him, however, was his determination—determination not only to survive, but also to escape."

explain next the concerns and apprehensions of the person conducting the interview.

- *Change times.* If you cannot think of anything more to say about the current aspects of your topic, tell readers how it was handled in the past or how it may be handled differently in the future.
- *Switch settings.* If you've explained how an event will have an impact on society as a whole, describe how it will affect your state, your country, your city, your neighborhood. Will it have an international impact?
- *Put on some background music.* Don't consciously stop working to listen to music, but put on a tape that may raise your spirits. Maybe the theme music from an exciting movie will stimulate you or the sounds of a string quartet will soothe your anxiety. Changing your mood may rechannel your thinking processes.
- *Reduce distractions.* Maybe you don't have writer's block at all. Perhaps the loud radio in the next apartment or the jackhammer tearing up the sidewalk in front of your house or the constant ringing of your telephone is keeping you from concentrating. Find a new place to work; use an answering machine to avoid interruptions; write at night when it is quiet, and sleep with ear plugs during the day. Do whatever you can to reduce distractions.
- *Set a time limit.* Don't feel any pressure to write for long, uninterrupted periods of time. After two hours, take a break. This will make you more productive when you resume your work.
- *Share the burden.* If you have a coauthor, send what you've written so far to him or her and say, "I'm stuck. Any ideas?" If you don't have a coauthor, take your problems with you to your next writers' club meeting and seek help. (In the meantime, turn your attention to a different writing project, but keep writing *something*.)
- *Remember past successes.* If you are depressed, look at your files containing your published articles and remind yourself that you *know* you can write publishable articles. You did it before, and you will do it this time, too.
- *Make an outline.* If you are blocked because you cannot see your writing project as a whole, jot down the key elements of what you need to focus on. Organize them in a logical sequence. Now, write something (even a few paragraphs) about each one in turn.
- *Get in the writing mode.* Try writing at the same time of day and in the same setting. A children's author once told us that she wrote daily from 5 a.m. to 7 a.m., in a straightback chair, with a yellow legal pad and a fountain pen filled with black ink (blue ink didn't work for her). In that situation, the words flowed easily.

Writer's block seems to be less of a problem for experienced writers than beginners. No, the work doesn't get any easier—writing is always difficult— but contracts, assignments, and deadlines create an urgency that motivates writers to keep writing. Putting words on paper is no longer a hobby, it's a

Rewrite/Revision

The following paragraph contains 75 words. Without sacrificing meaning or style, tighten and edit until you have reduced the word count by at least a third. The second paragraph is an edited version.

He came into the room without making any noise and went over to his grandmother with a certain amount of reluctance. The old woman looked away from him with an extremely sad face. He was sure she was about to speak to him. While he waited he thought about the many happy visits that he had made to this very house when he was a small boy. Still his grandmother kept silent and said nothing.

He entered the room noiselessly. With reluctance, he approached his elderly grandmother. She looked away, saddened, saying nothing. He waited, remembering his many happy visits as a boy to the house.

Revise the following passage by reworking the clichés into fresh images of your own choosing. The second paragraph is an example.

The morning dawned crystal clear and I was feeling frisky as a pup. For a moment I lingered under the covers, warm as toast, before touching one toe to the floor. It was cold as ice, but I decided to take the plunge anyway, and I scampered like a rabbit for slippers and robe.

The air was cold as I huddled under layers of warm covers. Gingerly I touched one bare foot to the icy floor. Brrr! I scampered for my slippers and robe.

business. If the writer hopes to stay in business, he has to have products already on the market and new products in various stages of development. In short, if the muse refuses to report for work at the appointed hour, give her a pink slip and go it alone. You may be surpised—even pleased—at the results.

Phase Three:
Finding Your Niche

Finding Your Niche

"You can survive as a writer on hustle: You get very little for each piece, but you write a lot of pieces."

—Kurt Vonnegut

Not long ago, three travel writers huddled in the corner of a Key West restaurant comparing notes by flashlight. The power had gone out again (a common occurrence on the island), and the writers had little to do but bemoan their next day's departure and the work that awaited them at home. They took turns answering this question: "What project tops your list?"

"A diet book, on a very tight deadline."

"A couple of consumer pieces for a computer magazine."

"An article-sidebar package about senior citizens who launch second careers."

Oddly, no one mentioned travel articles. Yet if anyone had inquired about their occupations, all would have responded "travel writer." Why? Because on that day, a Saturday, they were in the Keys to write travel articles; so, they were travel writers. Not until Monday would one of them become a nutrition expert, the second a technical writer, and the third a business reporter.

Only the most established of free lancers enjoy the luxury of writing in a specialized field. While many writers prefer certain areas of specialization and may be more proficient in some genres than others, generally, they write what editors buy. At any given time, the same writer might be researcher, reviewer or reporter. The willingness to tackle a variety of forms—often simultaneously—is what separates amateurs from professionals. Hobbyists write what they want to; the professionals write what they are assigned or can sell.

In this section of the book we will introduce you to several writing specialties in demand in editorial offices across the country. Success in each area
depends on two factors:
- your overall ability to write well
- your knowledge of the nuances of the specialty

As you experiment with various genres, you'll learn their special requirements and characteristics. For example, writing for inspirational markets
may not pay well, but most editors of religious publications buy only first
rights and encourage you to try to get your article reprinted in other non-
competing periodicals. You'll also discover that health articles need to be
marketed as quickly as possible before a new treatment or medication cuts
short your submission's shelf life. And, while major travel magazines tend
to use seasoned writers, editors of newspaper travel sections are always
looking for new voices.

Professional writers generally juggle from three to five projects simultaneously. Such an approach guarantees them that if one project is at a stand-
still (perhaps you're waiting for an interviewee to return your call), you can
turn your attention to a second project. One project often will stimulate
you to tackle another, and you can plan to alternate work on a heavy topic
with work on a light piece. Try to have your projects in different stages of
development. You may be sketching out an early outline for Project A,
writing a query for Project B, conducting interviews for Project C, and
working on a final draft of Project D. Such scheduling increases the chances
that Project D will appear in print the same time that Project A is entering
the research phase, Project B is being written to an editor's specifications,
and Project C is ready for submission to an editor who agreed to read it
on speculation.

Travel Writing

While "working vacation" might seem to be a memorable oxymoron, it
is surely no label for a writer on the road. Writers can't be on the job and
on vacation simultaneously. They're *either* tourists out for a good time *or*
they're writers out for a good article. Different hats. Different roles.

As an example, a writer spent two weeks in Spain on vacation. For 12 days
she was a typical tourist who sampled too much *paella*, was overwhelmed by
too many El Grecos, and bought too many souvenirs. Then, for two days,
she switched from tourist to professional, broke away from her group, took
a side trip to Gibraltar, shot a half dozen rolls of film, collected a shopping
bag full of materials, and interviewed several locals. Later, she rejoined the
group and resumed her vacation mode. When she returned home, she
wrote and sold the Gibraltar article not once, but twice. (See the Gibraltar

[Sample Travel Query]

September 25, 19—

Editor
Publication
Address
City, state, zip

Dear Ms. _____:

When visitors to Spain's glitzy Costa del Sol have had their fill of flamenco and sangria, they drive the dusty road that links Gibraltar to Spain and enjoy a spot of tea and a change of pace.

Gibraltar has welcomed guests from the mainland since 1985 when England and Spain finally resolved their centuries-old spat. The barrier (called the "Garlic Wall") tumbled down, the border opened up, and the tourists trooped in to see Britain's smallest and pluckiest royal outpost. It proved to be a bloody good show; so good, that the Rock currently plays host to more than four million visitors a year.

What tourists experience on a side trip to tiny "Gib" is veddy British indeed. Here, residents read London tabloids in pubs named Trafalgar Tavern, Old Vic and the Angry Friar; they cheer the cricket scores on the BBC; and they wash down their fish and chips with pints of stout. Old-timers trade memories of the queen's last visit in 1954, get misty over the motherland they've never seen, and credit Winston Churchill with protecting their Rock during the war not with arms but with apes. (More about *that* later.)

May I send you—on speculation, of course—a short article about Gibraltar? The Rock is the perfect side trip for Iberia-bound travelers who want to sample two cultures (British and Spanish) that merge on a rugged fortress between two continents—Europe and Africa. Where else can you enjoy steak and kidney pie prepared by a chef named Pedro?

Sincerely,

Author's Signature

query letter on the previous page.) Working vacation? Yes and no. For two days she worked, and for 12 days she vacationed.

What's your angle?

Would-be travel writers too often limit themselves to destination pieces that offer an overview of an area's accommodations, sights, restaurants, landmarks, weather, and people. Such articles can be successful if the destination is fairly unknown and not too large, but more focused pieces have a better chance of catching an editor's eye and fancy. Let's concentrate on five favorites that have an edge on traditional destination articles. These include travel with a twist, calendar-related pieces, how-tos, roundups, and participatory travel articles.

Travel with a twist

The best way to define "travel with a twist" is to describe three articles that fall into the category. Here's a sampling of several such articles by free lancers:

• A walking tour of San Francisco centered on Sam Spade, the fictitious detective who lived and worked in that city. Tour participants met under a lamppost (most of them appropriately dressed in trench coats) to visit spots around town that were popular haunts of Dashiell Hammett's famous sleuth. More than a destination piece about San Francisco, this article had a literary twist for fans of author Dashiell Hammett.

• A fantasy vacation prompted by the popular film *City Slickers* took East Coast sophisticates on a wagon-train trek across Wyoming. They cooked over open fires, slept on the ground, and bathed in icy lakes. More than an overview of Wyoming, this piece had the added dimension of city folk experiencing life without phones, fax machines, or indoor plumbing.

• Park City, Utah, a winter wonderland and home of America's Olympic ski team, was visited in the off season. The twist: What did tourists do when the lifts ground to a halt, the slopes weren't packed with snow, and iced tea replaced hot toddy as the drink of choice?

Editors like travel-with-a-twist articles because the pieces are two-dimensional and often unpredictable. The destination element is present, but it serves more as a backdrop and less as a focus. The real focus is the "twist" that teaches, entertains, or surprises the reader. Writers interested in producing travel-with-a-twist pieces would do well to choose subjects they know (Sam Spade mysteries, for example) and then select an appropriate setting. Other illustrations: A Mozart buff might lead readers on a tour of "Mozart's Vienna"; a sports fan might look at Sydney, Australia, as the host city of the 2000 Olympics; a wine connoisseur might offer pointers on the great red wines of France while toasting France's Burgundy region from a posh river barge.

Calendar-related articles

A calendar-related travel article is another option available to writers seeking relief from traditional destination pieces. (See also "Cyclical Marketing" in Phase Four.) This category includes seasonal stories—Oktoberfest in Munich, maple-sugar time in Vermont—as well as articles that highlight anniversaries and celebrations. The secret is to stay ahead of the calendar and know well in advance that, for example, 1992 was the 500th anniversary of the discovery of America and every town named Columbus would stage some kind of celebration; that 1993 marked the 300th anniversary of the founding of the Amish sect and visits to Amish communities in Pennsylvania, Ohio, and Indiana would yield great text/photo packages; and that 1994 was the 50th anniversary of D-Day and all newspapers and magazines would be revisiting the beaches of Normandy and talking to veterans who were part of the historic landing. Plans are now under way for a January 8, 2000, birthday bash in Memphis for Elvis Presley's 65th birthday.

One of the advantages of calendar-based articles is that a commemoration can boost an otherwise ho-hum destination into the national spotlight. One free lancer pitched the idea of a feature on Abilene, Kansas, to the travel editor of a national magazine. Hardly a mecca of tourism, Abilene seemed an unlikely choice for the travel section of a widely circulated publication until the writer pointed out that Dwight Eisenhower grew up in Abilene and that the following year would be the centennial celebration of Ike's birth. The calendar tie-in suddenly made the idea viable. The author was encouraged to write 750 words (one magazine page) and secure photographs of the Eisenhower family home and the presidential museum. Result? Her first byline in a major periodical.

The venerable how-to

The how-to article, a mainstay of many magazines, is particularly suitable for travel sections. Marketable ideas include how to choose luggage, how to pack, how to find low airfares, how to beat jet lag, how to travel with toddlers, and how to dicker with vendors. The seasoned writer tries for the unpredictable; for example, one writer did a piece on how to make the most of an airport layover. Written while the author was delayed at O'Hare Airport in Chicago and geared to the business traveler, it listed a dozen tasks that can be completed between flights. The writer's stopover proved to be lucrative: The piece sold to *Gulfshore Life, Fort Wayne Today, Market Builder,* and *Roto.*

The roundup

Look for a common thread—the most relaxing spas in America, the five best seafood restaurants on Cape Cod, 10 family vacations under $500— and use it to pull together several destinations. One creative writer who traveled cross country looking for Paradise in the USA, found not one but

20 cities and towns named Paradise and was able to parlay that bit of trivia into a delightful feature. A less whimsical and more straightforward article was produced by two writers who collaborated on a roundup of the best theme parks in America, an easy sale for a June issue of a family magazine.

Superlatives are important to roundup stories: the *most* remote campgrounds, the *best* dude ranches in the West, the *fastest* roller coasters, the *friendliest* bed-and-breakfast inns. Some tips to keep in mind as you scout for roundups: Don't try to survey too many destinations (three to five are enough), look for examples that are located in different parts of the country and suit a variety of budgets. Each component should be distinct from the others. No clones allowed.

Participatory travel

Often called adventure travel or ecotravel, participatory trips appeal to those with a fondness for active, rather than passive, entertainment. Adventure comes in degrees and ranges from easy to rigorous. Common to all is *involvement*. As an example, easy travel includes crossword-puzzle cruises hosted by the creator of a well-known series of puzzles. Participants circle their deck chairs and share dictionaries. Or, fans of French cuisine are invited to cook side by side with the great chefs of Europe. Each day begins with a trip to the local market and ends with a multi-course meal prepared by the group. In a more rigorous adventure, vacationers join the crew of a windjammer off the coast of the Bahamas or Maine, bike from inn to inn along the Connecticut coast, or lead a team of dogs across the Yukon.

To increase your chances of a sale, include with your participatory-travel article a sidebar that presents another adventure that can be enjoyed at the same destination. For example, one author wrote a behind-the-scenes story about a nationally known youth circus that performs annually in Peru, Indiana. She helped the clowns apply their makeup and shadowed the ringmaster between shows. During her interviews, she learned that the city had another claim to fame—it was the birthplace of songwriter Cole Porter. For a sidebar, she walked through Porter's old neighborhood, located his home, and visited his grave. Although the sidebar had nothing to do with the circus, with a clever title—"Where Cole Porter Began the Beguine"—it helped create a salable package, especially in 1993, Porter's 100th birthday.

When to query

Travel writers rarely leave home without some encouragement from an editor that their trip will result in an article sale. Unless you are a regular contributor to a publication's travel section, you probably won't have a firm assignment tucked inside your luggage when you board your plane, train, or cruise ship. The best you can hope for is encouragement from one or more editors. Incidentally, if you can convince them to express this interest in writing, you can in turn convince the IRS that you had good reason to believe that the articles you wrote about your trip would be published, and that was precisely why you took the trip. With good documentation, you may be able to claim your travel as a business expense whether your articles are accepted for publication or not.

The best time to query is *after* you've done preliminary research on your destination, yet *before* you embark on your journey. In your query, include your idea, your slant (twist? roundup? how-to?), and such nuts-and-bolts details as proposed length, availability of photos, and possible date of submission. Many travel writers also include with their query a postcard that will invite the editor to check one of the following responses:

_____ I would like to see your manuscript.

_____ This one isn't for us, but keep us in mind in the future.

_____ Thanks, but no thanks.

Some experienced travel writers prefer to take their trip without a secured assignment. Without encouragement from editors, they travel to their destination, come home, and dash off their query letters. This practice results in a good-news/bad-news situation. The good news is that your queries will be more colorful because you have experienced the sights and sounds of the destination and can communicate your enthusiasm in your letter. The bad news is that if editors don't share your enthusiasm, you must bear the cost of the trip with no hope of byline, payment, or tax deduction.

The final point at which you may query an editor is *after* the trip and *after* you have written your article. This is the mark of a true beginner, like a tailor who makes a suit and then scurries all over town to find a person the suit might fit.

Travel research techniques

Let's say you've secured enough encouragement from editors that you finalize your travel plans. The next step involves research—preliminary and on site. Pre-trip research generally involves visiting the library, collecting brochures from your local travel agent, buying a good guidebook and a current map. More important is the research you'll do after you reach your destination.

Travel journalists are notorious for taking few notes; instead, they look for shortcuts that allow them to enjoy their experience even as they collect the information to write a well-documented article. Instead of spending valuable time writing details in a notebook, seasoned travel writers know that a click of the shutter can preserve the same facts and impressions. We recommend two kinds of photos: publishable transparencies to offer to an editor and research snapshots to jog your memory, including photos of restaurants (inside and out), hotel rooms, plaques, and information signs. Postcards serve the same purpose, but with an extra advantage: You can scribble your impressions of a city or a landmark on the back of the postcard that depicts it.

Use a hotel's complimentary stationery to jot down your impressions of the establishment: Is the room clean? Attractive? Is the hotel located close to shopping and the theater district? How are the dining facilities? Is the staff courteous? This helps you differentiate between hotels when you move from one to another on a long trip. It also supplies the correct names, addresses, phone and fax numbers of the various stopovers for later use.

Keeping a daily journal is always a good idea, as long as you consider yourself more a color commentator than a play-by-play announcer. Instead of recording statistics and facts readily available in guidebooks and brochures, concentrate on your reactions and impressions. Sensations are also important: Taste the local food, take note of pollution levels, listen to the music and cadence of speech, be aware of sights to see or avoid. Is there a museum that should not be missed? An out-of-the-way pub that oozes charm? An abundance of pickpockets to be wary of in the city's square? Topless beaches that might shock the Elderhostel group from Des Moines?

Spend some time browsing through the yellow pages of the phone book. How many restaurants are listed? Are special accommodations available for persons traveling with young children or pets? Jot down the phone numbers of the local newspaper, commercial photographers, and the visitors' and tourist centers. These resources may come in handy if your photographs don't meet an editor's standards. Tourist centers often provide free color transparencies, although editors frequently veto them because they are widely distributed and may appear in other publications. If the editor wants to arrange for original photos, you can provide the phone numbers of the newspaper and local commercial studios.

One more tip: Collect props along the way. If you eat at a good restaurant, explain to the waiter that you are a travel writer and ask for a copy of the menu. If you enjoy an unusual bottle of wine at dinner, ask the manager to soak off the label and give it to you. You'll have not only the correct spelling of the winery but also vintage information. Plan to eat at a time when a restaurant isn't too busy. The staff will be more willing to visit with you then, and you'll be able to wander from room to room and snap pictures. Before you leave, pick up a matchbook that will list the address, phone number, and serving hours. And, before you check out of your hotel, be sure to request the manager's business card.

Hold the "I"

Beware of I-strain—first-person articles that too closely resemble written versions of home movies. Some editors are adamant that they will not consider "personal journeys" unless the traveler/writer is a celebrity. "Paul McCartney's Liverpool" or "The First Family's Weekend Hideaway" are sure bets for publication, but the Smiths' trip to the Wisconsin Dells is a certain throwaway.

Probably the best advice for newcomers to travel writing is to know the difference between a tourist and a travel journalist. As a writer, you have a responsibility to readers who may plan vacations based on your suggestions. Include enough whimsy to enchant and enough facts to inform your audience.

Book Reviewing

A free lancer's best chance of breaking into book reviewing is by contacting the book editor at a small weekly or mid-sized daily newspaper. Most of these publications devote one or two pages per week—often on Friday, Saturday or Sunday—to book reviews, a list of the current bestsellers, and interviews with and photos of authors passing through town on lecture tours. Reviews for these pages usually have a strict word count and follow a predictable format, with a first paragraph that gives the book's title, publisher, number of pages, and price, followed by a brief summary of the content and a reaction to the book.

Payment for most reviews is minuscule (as low as $30 for a 150- to 200-word review in a small newspaper), especially when you consider the number of hours required to read the book, make notes on its strengths and weaknesses, and then write a succinct appraisal. Also, unless you have a special arrangement with book publishers or magazine/newspaper editors to provide you with prepublication copies, you'll have to buy the book or borrow it from the library, and by that time it is too old for inclusion in a review section. Indeed, if a title is currently on the best-seller list, it is well past the review stage.

Typically, an editor will receive early copies of books (uncorrected pages, or soft-bound versions still not proofread) that will be sent to regular reviewers. The secret, then, is to contact a magazine editor, send along a sample of your writing, and offer to write a review on speculation. This can also work well if you are waiting to break into print by writing reviews for your local newspaper. In your cover letter, point out your areas of expertise or special interest that would qualify you to write credibly on a particular topic or genre. For example, if you are a fan of suspense novels and have read all of Mary Higgins Clark's books, use that as a selling point. The editor may think of you the next time a Clark thriller arrives at her office.

Three types of book reviews generally appear in magazines and newspapers: specialized reviews for specialized publications; long, essay reviews, such as those published in *The New York Times Book Review* or *The Washington Post Book World;* quick appraisals that are needed in great quantity by small weekly or mid-sized newspapers that produce weekly book pages.

Specialized reviews, as the name suggests, appear in publications read by an audience with common interests or in similar professions. For example, *CompuServe Magazine* is mailed to the million-plus subscribers to the CompuServe Information Service. Its monthly book review page focuses on books about software and hardware products, the information highway and other electronic-communication topics. Each printed review is a short "teaser" for the full-text review that is available online. Anyone wishing to contribute a review to *CompuServe Magazine* not only needs a better-than-average knowledge of computers, but also must have access to the information service.

The long, essay-type reviews that are published in magazine supplements such as *The New York Times Book Review* require that the reviewer give an overview of other books about the same topic and other works by the same author. This can become a mind-boggling assignment in some instances. For example, anyone who reviewed Kenneth S. Lynn's 1987 acclaimed biography, *Hemingway,* would need to be familiar with Lynn's previous books, with the many published biographies of Hemingway, and with Hemingway's works. It is understandable why scholars often are recruited to review works linked to their areas of expertise.

As rewarding as reviewing is in itself, it can lead to other, more lucrative assignments. For example, if you prove to be a dependable and knowledgeable reviewer, the book-page editor may eventually ask you to do a profile of a visiting author. Depending on the fame of the author, you may be able to recycle the profile by offering it to a magazine editor. One writer's first national byline was the result of just such a procedure. She interviewed Erma Bombeck for a small midwestern daily, was able to get enough quotable material from Bombeck to enable her to sell the article to the Associated Press, and then she recycled it a second time and sold it to a monthly magazine. What's more, Bombeck was pleased with the articles and later agreed to give the author two additional in-depth interviews.

Reading for pleasure is much different from reading for review. To hone your skills as a reviewer, select a familiar book (fiction or nonfiction) and work through the exercise on the facing page. After you've completed the checklist, write a review of 300 words (one typewritten page) in the style used on the book page of a newspaper or magazine that you have targeted.

Finding Fillers

If you want to ease your way into free-lance writing on a part-time basis, as most nonfiction writers do, consider the market for fillers and short items.

Fillers are informative or entertaining items of fewer than 250 words.

Book Review Checklist

Basic information:

Jot down the book's title, author, publishing house, copyright date, number of pages, price. Is it hardbound or paperback? Are there illustrations? Photos? Any other distinguishing characteristics?

For nonfiction:

What are the author's credentials for writing the book? His previous credits?

How in-depth was the author's research?

How is this book different from other books written about the same topic? What new concepts/ideas (or fresh approaches to familiar ideas and concepts) are presented?

What type of reader would find this book particularly beneficial?

Would you recommend this book? Why? Why not?

For fiction:

How does this book compare in theme and quality to the author's earlier works?

Does the book fit into a genre? Is it part of a series? A sequel to another book?

Write a two- or three-sentence summary of the plot.

Comment on the main characters. Are they realistic? Likable? How is the dialogue?

Does the story move at a pace that holds the reader's interest without confusing him?

Does the conclusion satisfy the reader? Does it leave any unanswered questions?

Would you recommend this book? Why? Why not?

They may include a recipe for *Woman's Day,* an anecdote for *American Legion Magazine,* or an inspirational thought for *Guideposts.* Payment for such items runs from $10 to $400, but an average payment is about $35.

Short items are mini-articles of 250 to 1,000 words that focus on one topic and offer opinions or information about it. Payment for these can range from $25 to $1,000, but the average is about $150. Sometimes fillers are used as sidebars or stand-alone supplements to longer features.

Many editors encourage free lancers to send a steady stream of articles of 1,000 words or fewer. They can be read and evaluated quickly. If purchased, they are used to fill odd half- or quarter-page spots in the issue being laid out. Many times, a magazine's advertising department has the opportunity to sell an advertisement late in an issue's production schedule. Although publishers welcome the additional revenue, editors cringe at the odd hole that such a late ad can create on a page. Having a ready supply of fillers solves such problems. Besides, editors know that readers enjoy short articles that can be read quickly in a dentist's waiting room or during coffee breaks at work.

To write a filler or short item, make a list of whatever you can discuss off the top of your head. Items may be nostalgic, a personal opinion about an issue, or a recommendation of how to handle a task more efficiently. Keep it snappy, obvious, easy to follow, and concise.

Focus on topics that will be of most importance to the reader: the benefits, the costs, the materials required, the time involved, the people concerned. If you need specific data that you don't know offhand, check an almanac or encyclopedia for general information. For more current facts, check the *Encyclopedia of Associations* (Gale Research Co.) for an association that can answer your questions.

Once your draft is completed, review it and eliminate extra examples or anecdotes that illustrate the same point more than once. Stay on one topic. If the text gets too involved, break your longer feature into two shorter ones, i.e., past/present or people/products or cars/trucks and so forth.

Virtually anything of interest as conversation qualifies as a potential topic to cover in a short item. Here are some general categories:

● *Places*—unique restaurants, bizarre museums, bargain family tours, offbeat art galleries.

● *Hobbies*—cow riding, cartooning, marble shooting.

● *Seasonal*—beating post-Christmas blahs, dyeing Easter eggs, fireworks safety reminders for Independence Day, gift ideas for the new graduate.

● *Business tips*—buying briefcases, hiring secretaries, choosing fax machines.

● *Short profiles*—prison guard, taxidermist, clown.

● *Miscellaneous*—recipes, crafts, family projects, games.

Your primary markets for fillers and short items will be small-circulation

Topics for Fillers and Short Items

- Security for garages and car ports
- Reducing postage costs
- Unusual ways to get to work (skateboard, rollerblades)
- How employees use coffee breaks
- What the company logo means
- Beating job boredom
- It's harder if you're left-handed
- Why I refinanced my home
- A telephone operator's funniest experiences
- Zany office regulations of major companies
- Suggestions on how to drive in bad weather
- Our week with a foster child
- Why Americans resisted metric changeovers
- Preparing for pregnancy leave
- Weekend warriors: National Guardsmen on duty
- Local speakers' bureaus
- Is early retirement a good idea?
- How to shop a flea market
- Contemporary office jargon
- How to winterize your home
- The effect of calculators on teaching math
- Statistics about smoke alarms

magazines, Sunday newspaper supplements, company publications, and general consumer periodicals.

Make a List, Write an Article!

List articles are straightforward, and follow a three-part basic format: a lead paragraph that explains the focus of the list and its usefulness; the list itself (always using a specific number of points, each supported by anecdotes, quotations and facts); and the ending that either summarizes the article or motivates/challenges the reader to use the list's suggestions or plans or informative data.

If you were to tour your house right now to take a survey of the various articles you have clipped from publications, you would discover that most are list articles. There they are, taped inside medicine cabinets ("Five Ways to Counteract Household Poisons"), wedged into the side of bedroom mirrors ("Eight New Approaches to Hair Styling"), or attached to the refrigerator door with magnets ("Six Emergency Numbers Your Babysitter Should Know"). List articles grab people's attention and intrigue readers because they offer promises: They promise to provide a specific number of ideas, solutions, tips, insights, or facts.

List articles are also entertaining. Readers are amused by lists of superlatives. They want to know what in the world is best, worst, cheapest, most expensive, youngest, oldest, hardest, softest, kindest, rudest, happiest, saddest, blandest, or spiciest. Readers have an innate curiosity about what they might be missing in life; list articles address that curiosity.

Many times ideas for list articles can come from your friends. Listen carefully to what people complain about, and then try to discover a series of solutions to those frustrations.

If your neighbor complains about employee theft in his company, you can write "Ten Tips For Controlling Internal Theft" and offer it to a business periodical. If your pastor mentions the difficulty of getting church members to arrive on time for Sunday morning services, you can write a feature for denominational magazines called "Five Ways to Get 'Em to the Church on Time." If your grandmother says she feels lonely, you can write "Seven Ways to Brighten a Senior Citizen's Day" for a general interest, family, or religious periodical.

Probably the best reason to try your hand at list articles is that they are extremely easy to write. They require no special knowledge on the author's part and only a minimum amount of research (much of which can be obtained by telephone). Often they are culled from leftover material you've gathered for another article. For example, after completing an article about characteristics of successful entrepreneurs, an author, reviewing her notes in search of possible spinoff article ideas, was struck by the number of failures that her interviewees had had on the way to becoming successful. This led to an article called "Seven Ways to Respond to Failure" that focused on the lessons failure can teach. A women's magazine snapped it up.

Keep in mind that lists are more functional than stylistic. As such, you can merely present your material in sequential order. Just give the facts. Nothing else is needed.

The Personal Experience Article

Pretend for a moment that you are an editorial assistant at a magazine, and one of your duties is to read the unsolicited manuscripts that arrive daily at your office. Because your time is limited, you rarely read a submission in its entirety. You read until you lose interest, then you slip a printed rejection slip under the paper clip, and return the manuscript. Say that on this particular day you receive two articles dealing with mid-life divorce.

Potential "List Articles" About Your Home Town

- The four most expensive animals at the city zoo
- Six unidentifiable items found in an antique store
- Our library's ten most-requested classic books
- The five oldest businesses on Main Street
- The ten oldest tombstones in the village graveyard
- Four pediatricians share their funniest experiences
- Profiles of three husband-wife business teams
- Five politicians reveal their New Year's resolutions
- Nine ways to reduce local taxes
- The eight best days to visit your child's school
- Four pie recipes from retired pastry chefs
- Three reasons for spending your vacation at home
- Seven ministers' wives discuss child rearing
- Six obscure landmark plaques revealed locally
- The three most dangerous intersections in town

Each is written from the point of view of the author, a woman. Based on the opening paragraph, which manuscript would you reject immediately, and which would you continue reading?

> We were married on September 25, 1964, in a lovely ceremony at the First Presbyterian Church on Grand Avenue in Detroit. I remember how handsome Chad looked in his black tuxedo with the red cummerbund that matched the dozen roses I carried. I had three attendants, including my sister, Pat, who is five years older than I. Pat and I are very close. . . .

***

> Bill came home late that night, and I knew he had something on his mind as soon as he walked into the kitchen. "I want a divorce," he said bluntly.

If you work for a magazine that never publishes personal-experience articles—and many periodicals have such a policy—you will automatically reject both submissions. Otherwise, you probably will reject the first manuscript after reading the lead paragraph, and you'll reserve judgment on the second article until you've sampled more of it. Why? The author of the first article has committed two errors found in many personal-experience articles. First, she starts her article with her marriage ceremony rather than at the beginning of the critical point of her story. Second, she includes far more detail than the reader needs (or wants) to know. The author of the second article wastes no time in plunging the reader into the drama of the story, and enhances the impact of Bill's announcement by omitting all unnecessary descriptions and explanations leading up to it.

On the surface, writing about a personal experience may seem easy. It requires little research, the author can provide vivid descriptions, and the process of writing can, in itself, be cathartic. We've all heard the advice that says the best way to work out a problem is to work through it. One way to work through a painful memory is to write down the events and feelings related to it, then to step back and try to view them objectively. What a bonus if such a helpful exercise also yields a free-lance sale!

A word of caution: The disadvantages of publishing personal experiences may outweigh the advantages. It may be painful for you to relive memories, and writing honestly about the past forces you to share your vulnerability, weaknesses, and shortcomings with the world. Writers find it difficult to portray themselves objectively. They either gloss over their weaknesses or are too critical of their actions. And, the example cited above shows that an author may be tempted to recount the memory in chronological order, without omitting the tiniest detail. The result is often too graphic, too long, and too boring for anyone who was not directly involved in it.

Add to these "negatives" the fact that your personal experiences probably involve other people—relatives, friends, colleagues, associates, or a spouse. How will they react to seeing themselves in print—embarrassed? angry? Will it cause a rift in your relationship? Will it harm anyone's reputation? Could the person sue you for invasion of privacy? If the answer to the last question is "yes," you had better obtain written permission from the person mentioned in the article. Your other options are to fictionalize your story or to alter the characterizations of key players to make them unrecognizable.

These sobering words of caution are not meant to deter you from writing in the first person. Some articles are best told from the author's point of view, and the drama of an event is surely heightened when the reader knows that the account is true. Article writers—particularly newcomers to the free-lance ranks—should understand that point of view is a choice. They must decide if they want to be objective spectators (using third-person) or active participants (speaking in first-person) in the personal experience articles they plan to tell and sell.

To help you identify experiences that might be marketable as first-person articles, read the list of "Turning Points" on the next page. Before developing a turning point into an article, ask yourself five questions about the experience:

● Will readers be able to identify with my account and learn from its solution?

● Does my article have a beginning, a middle and an end?

Turning Points

Persons who write from their own experience often search their lives for "turning points"—key moments that are life-changing. Focus on pivotal events in your past by filling in the blanks of these sentences. Review your answers. Can any turning point be developed into a first-person article?

A setback that helped me grow was _____
_____
_____.

An important lesson my parents taught me was _____
_____
_____.

The best advice anyone ever gave me was _____
_____
_____.

I knew I was an adult when I _____
_____
_____.

The greatest risk I ever took was _____
_____
_____.

The most serious mistake I *almost* made was _____
_____
_____.

The toughest challenge I ever faced was _____
_____
_____.

The hardest goodbye I ever said was _____
_____
_____.

The most memorable gift anyone ever gave me was _____
_____
_____.

- Will the telling of my experience embarrass me or anyone close to me?
- What is my motivation for writing this piece?
- Has enough time passed that I can be objective and honest?

The first two questions will be of interest to any editor you approach. Readers are always looking for articles with "take-away" value. Although the account is uniquely yours, readers will hope to find some lesson they can draw from it and apply to their own lives. They also want a complete account with a short introduction (begin just as the "something" is about to happen), a description of the problem, and a resolution to the problem. Writers must beware of writing their articles too soon after the events have occurred. Determining your motivation for writing the article will help you know if your timing is right: Writing to help your readers is a healthy motivation; writing just to help yourself is not. Again, getting something off your chest may be therapeutic, but it probably should be done in therapy rather than in print.

As you look for likely markets for your personal-experience pieces, take note of publications that seem to have a bias in favor of or against first-person voice. Watch for magazines that have front-of-the-book and back-of-the-book features that actively solicit personal stories. Sometimes these articles are opinion or "speaking-out" pieces of about 1,000 words that allow writers to vent their feelings about important issues. Other publications—*Guideposts,* for example—specifically want firsthand accounts of how you dealt with a contemporary problem or situation and solved it.

Taking Humor Seriously

In his essay "What's So Funny?" James Thurber set out to explain how to be a humor writer. The assignment proved to be so difficult, he wound up writing 3,000 words on what sorts of things definitely were *not* funny. Along the way, Thurber implied that there were no proven formulas that would guarantee laughs from readers.

Professional humor writers will tell you that the most difficult aspect of their work is creating something that will be funny to a wide audience and will spark a laugh months after publication. A series of jokes about riding in big-city cabs might be hilarious to a Wall Street stockbroker, but not to a farmer in Iowa. Conversely, a long-winded yarn about a city slicker trying to figure out how to drive a tractor might delight the Iowa farmer, yet cause the New York stockbroker to lift his hands and say, "I don't get it." A political satirist might garner laughs for his column about Washington politics, but when he tries to include the material in an anthology, he finds that few readers recall the targets of his barbs.

Stand-up comics who perform for convention crowds spend weeks ahead of time getting information about what the conventioneers make, advertise, ship, and sell. This allows the entertainers to aim their humor at the particular interests of the audience. And that's the key to writing and selling humor: Don't write the piece first and then hope to find a periodical that will buy it; rather, study the periodical and then write something that you think will be funny to that magazine's specific readership. Also read the ads to get a feel for the tone of the publication.

One experienced humor writer says that his favorite approach to comedy is to imagine "what if" scenarios. For example, the editor of *Stereo* asked him to write something funny related to music. To get ideas, he started leafing through books about famous composers and happened across a full-length drawing of Beethoven.

It struck the writer that with his long hair, his long black overcoat and shiny black boots, Beethoven looked a lot like country-music singer Johnny Cash. The writer concluded that, based on looks alone, Beethoven could probably land an audition in Nashville if he were alive today. But, would Beethoven be impressive enough to secure a record contract? Speculating on this, he wrote, "Could Beethoven Have Made It In Nashville?" which the editors and readers of *Stereo* found hilarious.

This same writer was surprised to discover that poet Robert Frost (1874–1963) was born two years before novelist and short-story writer Jack London (1876–1916). Because London became world-famous when he was only twenty-one and Frost did not publish his first collection of poems until he was thirty-nine, as a fledgling writer Frost might have turned to London for advice. The result was an article, "If Jack London Had Edited Robert Frost," which pretended to have London edit Frost's poem, "Stopping by Woods on a Snowy Evening." The fact that the writers were contemporaries made it believable; the fact that they were totally opposite in their approaches to describing nature made it funny. Each time Frost would insert a line about how "lovely, dark and deep" the woods were as the snow drifted down, London would delete the description and scribble a line about avalanches and blizzards.

So, if you want to try your hand at humor, just imagine "what if" scenarios. On one side of a piece of paper write the names of twenty famous people (Confucius, Betsy Ross, Mahatma Gandhi, Albert Einstein, Mickey Mantle, Sandra Day O'Connor, Al Gore, Dave Letterman, etc.) and on the other side list 20 contemporary occupations (computer programmer, used-car salesman, astronaut, fashion consultant, sports commentator, etc.).

Now, mix and match. What would happen if, say, Gandhi were a used-car salesman? His sales pitch might include a phrase such as "I'm completely honest, sir. I'd give you the shirt off my back, but as you can see, I don't have one." (Remember as you create such lines that there is a difference between what is funny and what is just silly. A joke or scene that makes a reader snicker or groan is not humorous, it's just ridiculous.)

This mix-and-match game can go on endlessly. A variation calls for focusing on "situations" rather than "occupations," such as James Thurber's "If Grant Had Been Drunk at Appomattox." Use your imagination.

Another approach to humor is to create surprise. This involves writing a sentence or two that seems to be saying one thing, but suddenly turns out to have a totally unexpected (and funny) different meaning ("Take my wife . . . please").

A good example of the use of surprise is found in Louis Sachar's *Sideways Stories from Wayside School* when he writes, "Nancy had big hands and big feet. And he didn't much like his name either." Another example is the late Jackie Vernon's line, "My grandfather was an old Indian fighter and my grandmother was an old Indian." Another line comes from Woody Allen, who said, "I sometimes get so depressed, I want to revert to the womb. Anyone's." In each example, there is an unexpected twist at the end.

A variation on the joke or one-liner surprise is the "sight gag" surprise. For example, a man is walking down the street reading a newspaper. A banana peel is a few feet ahead of him. Just before he reaches it, he glances down and spots the banana peel. Cautiously, he steps around it and backs away from it, keeping it in sight. Two steps later, he backs into an open manhole.

Think back to surprises in your life and make a list of them. Did you ever take a trip and wind up at the wrong location? Did you ever accidentally walk into the wrong room at a funeral parlor? Did you ever think it was Friday when it was only Thursday? Have you ever dialed the number of one friend thinking it was the number of another friend (who was at odds with the first friend)? Obviously, these "natural surprises" occur all the time. All you need to do is to build on them to create a funny story or scene.

Be careful not to belabor a funny incident. Some humor doesn't translate well into words: It's better seen than heard. A short "bit" of humor is better told as a joke or used as a filler item than stretched into a full-length humor piece. For instance, one writer friend described her visit to CBS for an interview with Andy Rooney. When she sat down in Rooney's office her chair collapsed beneath her, sending her sprawling on the floor. As Rooney calmly reached down to help her up, he instinctively launched into one of his *60 Minutes* monologues: "Did you ever wonder why they don't build chairs the way they used to?" She used this incident as a one-paragraph humorous lead for her article on Rooney, but not as an article.

There are many types of humor—dry, wry, witty, caustic, sarcastic, ironic, slapstick, situation comedy, satire, and one-liners. Whatever your specialty, here are some tips to guide you:

Writing Humor: Learning to See the Funny Side of Life

Humor is based on truth. Though exaggerated or satirized, humor should be based on situations readers can identify with. Many times an author uses standard expressions or common references to make the humor even more realistic to readers. Asking yourself these basic questions can help you decide what to have some fun with.

1. What irritates me most, and how can I describe it humorously?

2. What are my spouse's (or children's) weirdest habits? How can I depict them humorously?

3. What have I seen on television or in a newspaper lately that would be fun to parody?

4. What outrageous things would happen if I were to put two well-known but incredibly different people together on a desert island?

Make notes about each topic. What age, size, shape, color, taste, or weight is associated with the occurrence or situation? What behavior, habits, traditions, rules, laws, or skills apply to it? From these notes, imagine what might happen if you discussed it by using jokes, sarcasm, wit, parody, puns, spoofs, satire, exaggeration, tall tales, irony, slapstick, drollness, absurdity, and/or imitation.

When you've compiled enough funny one-liners, gags, funny scenes and satirical remarks, you can formulate them into a full-length article or short item.

• Keep it short. Trim your text to the minimum. Leave your readers wanting more. Most humor columns are fewer than 1,000 words.

• Stay in control. Sometimes, trying to be witty about a hot issue can produce great copy that readers relate to (politics, fashion, religion). But be careful it isn't offensive. Don't get so fired up that the humor melts away.

• Be up to date. Don't slip into clichéd humor. Some of the early sitcoms centered on stereotypes—ditzy housewives (*I Love Lucy*) or bumbling blue-collar types (*The Honeymooners*). They are classics; but you are contemporary. Make sure you have a new angle before you try reviving an old joke in print.

Most publications welcome good humor writing. It's always in demand, probably because there isn't enough to go around. It can't be manufactured; it has to be observed and recorded.

Being funny for money

There are numerous markets for humor. A good place to break into humor writing is a local small-town newspaper. Write three or four columns about things that you feel people in that area would find humorous. Submit the columns to the features editor, along with a list of 10 other humorous topics you could write about. Offer to write a weekly column. Keep copies of all your printed columns to help you try syndication later, and/or to collect them for possible publication in book form.

Greeting card publishers, ranging from Oatmeal to Hallmark, pay from $25 to $150 for witty sayings and ideas for greeting cards. Type your concept on a 3x5 card (one idea per card).

Cartoonists, too, need gag ideas. Submit them on a 3x5 card that explains the premise of the gag and the punchline. For example: Scene shows a plumber with the back off a toilet. A trout is leaping from the tank. The caption reads, "I think I found the source of your problem, Mrs. O'Malley." Marketing books carry listings of cartoonists seeking gags.

Stand-up comics also buy jokes from free-lance writers. It is usually best to prepare 30 to 50 jokes and either submit them to a well-known comic through his or her agent or to take the material directly to a comic who might be appearing at a comedy club or benefit. To contact a comic's agent, write to the Screen Actors Guild (SAG), 1515 Broadway, 44th Floor, New York, NY 10036; or the American Federation of Television and Radio Artists (AFTRA), 260 Madison Ave., New York, NY 10016.

Easy Sale: Wellness Features

Dr. Kenneth Cooper, wellness expert and the father of aerobics, estimates that 75 percent of disease in America is linked to unhealthy lifestyles, and 65 percent of premature deaths are preventable. These numbers translate into welcome news for health advocates and enormous opportunities for free-lance writers. Since readers know that good health often is a matter of choice rather than chance, they are receptive to a constant flow of information about how they can get and stay fit. Editors are aware of readership interest, and they're also aware of the dollars-and-cents value of including wellness features in their publications. Companies that sell products related to health and fitness are among the top 10 advertisers in magazines today, and they prefer to buy space in periodicals that publish articles that support their interests.

Free-lance writers can boost their chances of sales if they remember three pieces of advice: First, always emphasize wellness over illness (prevention over treatment). This gives readers a sense of empowerment; they assume an active rather than a reactive position. Second, under the category of "health," writers should include not only physical health, but also mental, emotional, and psychological health. This expands the range of viable topics to include coping with stress, overcoming depression, recognizing learning disabilities, building and maintaining relationships—and the list goes on and on. Third, writers should study a magazine's readership and focus on its particular health concerns. A senior citizens' magazine might be interested in an article about preparing well-balanced meals on a fixed income; a publication geared to corporate executives might buy a feature that examines the value of in-house fitness facilities for employees.

The innovative free lancer can give a health twist to almost every article. After producing a traditional travel piece about luxury cruise vacations, for instance, one writer recycled the material and came up with a second article that focused on shipboard exercise programs. A sidebar suggested heart-smart dinner entrees that passengers can request at no extra charge and also mentioned that special meals are available on airplanes. For an article about hobbies that appeal to adults, she interviewed a psychiatrist and a psychologist who discussed the emotional value of hobbies. The doctors agreed that high-powered executives need the kind of escape that an engaging pastime can provide. This angle appealed to the managing editor of a computer magazine whose readers are upwardly mobile males, ages 30 to 40, who typically work 60-hour weeks, often in front of a computer screen.

Certainly the challenges of writing wellness articles include keeping up with health trends and knowing when the reading public has overdosed on a topic. Anorexia, bulimia, toxic shock syndrome, and chronic fatigue syndrome have been covered thoroughly in the past decade. They're still important, but unless a writer has new information to present, editors may consider them to be yesterday's news. Two developments can make a topic timely again—a breakthrough in treatment or a well-known person going public with a health condition. When First Lady Betty Ford had breast cancer, most women's magazines explored every angle of the disease, from diagnosis to treatment options to support groups to prevention strategies. When former President Ronald Reagan revealed his Alzheimer's disease, publications featured interviews with doctors and researchers about the symptoms and treatments for the illness. When Oprah Winfrey lost, gained, and lost weight, interest surged in diet and fitness programs. Her personal chef shared recipes in a book—*In the Kitchen with Rosie*—that quickly climbed to the top of the best-seller list.

The easiest way to know if readers have tired of a wellness topic is to visit the periodical section of the library and make a list of recurring health-related subjects addressed in the major magazines. Also, take time to review newspaper reports about new research. Note the names of persons who are conducting new studies at universities and medical centers. Publications such as *American Demographics* magazine will provide information about health trends; *The New England Journal of Medicine* will offer up-to-date research data. Many almanacs list names, addresses, and telephone numbers of associations that compile and disseminate information about specific health conditions (example: Alzheimer's Disease and Related Disorders Association, Inc.).

On a less scholarly level, radio and television talk shows can give you insights as to what's new and of concern to their audiences—and maybe to yours. Often the topics that viewers first encounter on television will appear in print three to four months later. Indexes to *The New York Times,* found in large public libraries, provide references to articles about breakthroughs in many health-related subjects. Track down the articles and look for names of principal investigators and researchers of your topic.

As you gather general background information about wellness and fitness, check with the Consumer Information Center, Box 100, Pueblo, CO 81009. This agency distributes U.S. government publications on a range of subjects—from body wraps to varicose veins. Most are free, although some require a nominal fee. The material is very general, but it serves as a good launch point for your research. You can also write to the National Cancer Society, March of Dimes, Multiple Sclerosis Society of America, the American Lung Association, and other national groups to request that your name be added to their lists of writers to receive press releases and media kits. The *Public Relations Journal Register Issue* is an excellent guidebook of names and addresses of public relations professionals in the healthcare industry.

Two additional resources are available to authors who have access to fax machines, computers, and modems. The Centers for Disease Control and Prevention (CDC) now offers a CDC FAX Information Service, an automated system designed to help callers retrieve health information easily and quickly. The service is available 24 hours a day, 365 days a year, and provides information about a range of health issues, grouped by topic, each with a reference number for easy access. Also, the National Institutes of Health (NIH) sponsors a dial-in electronic bulletin board system that can be accessed directly, computer to computer, or through the Internet. Available files include lists of all NIH publications, press releases that describe newsworthy developments, feature articles written by NIH science writers, clinic alerts (announcements about biomedical research that have immediate implications), and articles prepared by the NIH that appeared in *The Journal of the American Medical Association.*

As helpful as these services are, they are merely your first step in gathering material about health-related topics. After securing basic information, you will be ready to progress to the most important phase of research—interviewing healthcare professionals, researchers, and patients. (This also applies to ideas in other fields.)

Unless you are a physician yourself, the information that you share with readers is only as credible as the sources (interviewees) who supply it. For national magazines, the experts you quote must have widespread professional authenticity. Where do you find such heavy hitters? Start with a local physician, ask for referrals, and then work up and out. If your quest leads you to a medical school faculty, ask for the head of a department, a full professor, a chief of staff, or someone who has published extensively on the topic. Always seek the person with the best credentials. All hospitals and medical centers of any size have full-time public relations staffs, among whose duties is accommodating interview requests from working writers.

As you gather information, seek second, third, and fourth opinions. Balancing one point of view with another guarantees an unbiased story and prompts readers to get involved and form their own opinions. As a safeguard against becoming academic and dull, include anecdotes, short case studies, and interviews with patients. A sidebar might take the form of a quiz that lets readers test their general medical knowledge and "grade" themselves against the answers you provide. Other sidebar possibilities include lists of do's and don'ts, symptoms, and warning signs.

Sometimes the human element is tougher to track than clinical data. Patients may not want to talk, or writers may get caught up in a subject's emotion and find it difficult to walk that fine line between the warmly personal and the intimate. You must be sensitive to patients and their problems, yet elicit enough personal information from them to make your article interesting without being sentimental . . . though a little sentiment is important.

Whatever the specific health-related topic, you'll have a better chance of selling your article if it has a hopeful (even if not necessarily happy) ending, emphasizes what's new in wellness research, and blends an explanation of what the researcher is doing in his laboratory with information on the potential benefit to readers.

How-to Articles

The single easiest article to write and sell today is the how-to article. It follows a no-frills, four-part formula that is in demand in almost every kind of magazine—specialized and general interest. The author who masters the basic formula can produce salable material for travel publications ("How to Beat Jet Lag"), sports magazines ("How to Improve Your Golf Game by Five Strokes"), religious markets ("How to Share Your Testimony With a Friend"), finance ("Saving for Retirement Painlessly"), and health periodicals ("How to Add Ten Years to Your Life"). Most magazines welcome how-to articles (they make great cover lines), and most topics can be readily reshaped to fit the how-to format. For example:

General topic	How-to article
Body language	"How to read between the lines"
Mental depression around the holidays	"How to cope with a blue Christmas"
Money-making strategies for writers	"How to earn more than pennies for your thoughts"
Stretching income to cover expenses	"How a single parent manages her money"
New England's regional cooking	"How to host the perfect clambake"

As an author of how-to articles, you will face two challenges. First, you must make sure that the articles you write truly deliver on their promise to teach readers something that they previously did not know; you should never repackage the obvious. Don't promise to share tips about how to lose weight, and then simply instruct readers to eat less and exercise more. Such "wisdom" makes readers feel they've been duped into buying the magazine and reading the article. They expected help, but instead were just tricked out of their money.

Second, you must make the directions you give easy to understand and follow. At the heart of every how-to article is a list of clearly defined steps, often numbered or set off by some simple typographical device (checkmarks, bullets, asterisks, etc.). If each step requires more than a few paragraphs to explain, your topic might be better covered in more than one article or in a book.

Most how-to articles teach readers how to improve something intangible (how to get along with your ex-in-laws) or create something tangible (how to make a quilt). Since we live in a society that is obsessed with self-improvement, the intangibles have the edge. Readers never seem to tire of advice that helps them manage, overcome, avoid or cope with daily problems. The tone of the articles is generally warm, the voice is usually second person (as the writer, you are chatting one-on-one with your friend, the reader), and the formula is familiar:

- Introduction
- Transitional sentence or paragraph
- Steps
- Closure (optional)

In the introduction, the author "bonds" with the reader by describing a common set of circumstances or telling an anecdote that the reader can relate to. Here's an example of how an article that aims to show readers how to make a speech without panicking might begin:

> Your heart was pounding as you took a final gulp of ice water and blotted your mouth with the napkin. *Breathe deeply,* you told yourself. *Inhale . . . one, two, three . . . exhale . . . one, two, three.* Why had you ever accepted the invitation to speak at the mother-daughter banquet?
>
> The waiter cleared the last dish from the head table, and the emcee began her introduction. There was no turning back. You were on.

After grabbing the reader's attention with this description, you quickly make a transition to the key point of the article—the advice you are sharing. The bridge from anecdote to advice can be made in three simple sentences.

> Survey after survey shows that most Americans fear public speaking more than they fear a new job or a major move. Yet, at some time or other, most of us are called on to mount a platform, with knees knocking and palms sweating, to "say a few words." Experts argue that this dreaded experience can be relatively painless if speakers follow five easy rules.

With the bridge built, you next present your five easy rules in a clip-and-save format (many readers will bypass the introduction, transition, and closure and cut and preserve only the "steps" for future reference). Each piece of advice is accompanied by an anecdote, a quotation from a well-known source, or an example that illustrates the point. A quick wrap-up paragraph brings the article to an effective conclusion.

Where to look for how-to ideas

Many would-be writers want to break into print but often overlook one of the best sources: writing how-to articles from their own experience. A geriatric nurse who dreamed of writing the great American romance novel chalked up a few bylines by addressing such salable topics as "How to Care for Aging Parents at Home," "How to Choose the Right Nursing Home," and "Ten Ways to Brighten a Senior Citizen's Day." (How-to articles don't always begin with the words "how to.") A mortician who wanted to write humor first established himself as a published author by writing "How to Cope with Grief" and "How to Plan a Funeral." A homemaker who labeled herself a "rummage sale junkie" offered tips on "How to Shop at Garage Sales" and sold versions of the manuscript to a hobby magazine, a periodical for owners of rental properties, and a newspaper's business page.

In addition to firsthand experiences, personal matters of concern sometimes produce good material for how-to articles. What issues are on your mind right now? Are you thinking about taking early retirement? Making a mid-life career shift? Going back to school? Relocating to another part of the country? Selling your house? Chances are, a lot of other people are wrestling with the same questions and would like help in finding solutions to them. Choose one topic and brainstorm. For example, if you are contemplating retirement, these questions might arise:

- Retirement: How to know when to go
- How to live on a fixed income
- How to choose a retirement community
- How to retire with financial security at age 50
- How to launch a second career after age 65

A third place to look for likely how-to topics is in the media. What are people discussing on the talk shows? What questions are they posing to advice columnists? There are numerous advice columns, such as "Ann Landers" and "Dear Abby" and "Ask Beth," as well as a variety of question-and-answer columns like those found in *Parade* and *The Star*, that respond to the concerns and interests of various age groups. What issues are dominating the news? With crime on everyone's mind, make a list of crime-prevention ideas, such as how to form a neighborhood association; how to safeguard your home; how to avoid becoming a victim; and how to protect yourself from car-jackings or being assaulted while walking your dog.

You don't have to be an expert before you offer advice in a how-to article, but the information you share must be credible and authoritative. If you are an authority on the topic you're discussing, you should state your credentials in the opening few sentences. For example, the funeral director who writes "How to Cope with Grief" needs to establish that he has counseled grieving families for 25 years; the geriatric nurse who writes "How to Choose the Right Nursing Home" needs to explain that she has cared for senior citizens for more than three decades.

If you are not an expert on a topic, you still can write about it and use a how-to format. Like any piece of nonfiction, you should identify, interview, and quote the best experts available. If your sources are credible, the information in your article will be accurate.

Selecting illustrations for a how-to article is a decision that rests with the editor; however, a writer can make suggestions. Articles that teach readers to create something tangible—a Christmas ornament, a gingerbread house,

How-To Article Worksheet

The purpose of my article is to:

_____ Instruct   _____ Inspire
_____ Explain   _____ Motivate

After finishing my article, readers will know how to _____
_____.

The steps through which I will walk my readers are:

1. _____.

2. _____.

3. _____.

4. _____.

5. _____.

Supplies, knowledge or preparation that my readers will need include: _____
_____
_____.

My article will be illustrated by (photos? graphics?):
_____
_____.

In my introduction, I will spark reader interest by:
_____
_____.

or new closet shelves that will make more room in your condo—usually require photographs or drawings that reinforce and clarify the text. Articles that deal with intangibles—how to improve a relationship, how to know when to retire—generally rely on illustrations produced or secured by the publication's art director, though a valid idea or concept for illustration from a writer is usually welcome.

To experiment with the how-to format, work through the exercise on the previous page. Remember to include an example, an anecdote or other supporting material for each step. Plan two articles—the first dealing with how to create a tangible object and the second focusing on how to create something intangible.

The Crossover Market

Active free-lance writers have numerous target markets for their manuscripts: secular and religious, trade and technical, hobby and professional, men's and women's, domestic and foreign, to mention but a few.

The secret to making a topic "cross over" from one type of market to another entirely different one—from the secular to the religious, for instance—is in finding a way to make the subject pertinent to the new market. An article on aerobic exercising can be sold to a variety of secular magazines. However, to make the same article appropriate for religious periodicals, one must show how aerobics can be synchronized with the recitation of Bible verses; or how aerobics can be incorporated into a vacation Bible school activity time or at a religious sponsored camp.

By carefully studying the guidelines for a variety of publications, writers can see how to modify versions of one article on quick-fix meals for working moms (for a women's magazine) into a new article (for a men's magazine) called "Easy Home-Cooked Meals Even a Bachelor Can Handle." Similarly, an article about television repair prepared for a technical magazine could be simplified and sold to a general interest magazine as, "Avoid a Service Call: Replace the Transistor Board in Your TV."

List topics you could write about and challenge yourself to come up with article ideas that would work for divergent markets. For example, a senior citizens' article, "Keeping Grandkids Occupied," could be retooled for young parents into "Tips on Helping at Your Child's Nursery" (same material, new slant). Or, "Planning the Family Picnic" (secular marketplace) could become "Outdoor Fun for Church Groups" (religious marketplace).

The benefit of writing for the crossover markets is that the original research a writer does for any article will remain valid. What will change is the format or the style of writing used to present this material. That's where discerning the needs of a particular periodical's readers will be crucial to a writer. If the writer learns how to "speak" to those readers, he will find a ready market for his manuscript.

Profiles

Any kind of writing that you do—nonfiction, humorous or serious, historical or contemporary—involves creating profiles. In all nonfiction, you describe the people involved. Sometimes, in the case of a round-up article, you may quote several people and each brief "profile" is little more than a snapshot. You quote a person and quickly establish who he or she is as part of the attribution.

In the case of a fully developed personality profile, you present a detailed portrait of the person. Depending on your style of writing and the requirements of the editor, this might be a very flattering "illustration" of your interviewee (think of a photograph that has been touched up to eliminate all imperfections). Or, it might be what many journalists call a "warts and all" likeness (a photo that clearly reveals every blemish, freckle, and age line). The "warts" phrase merely suggests that the author-interviewer presents a balanced picture and points out the person's shortcomings as well as his attributes.

Although the trend today is toward the "warts and all" profile and biography, some editors still believe that if you can't say something nice about somebody, you shouldn't say anything at all. In an interview for *The Saturday Evening Post,* country-music star Barbara Mandrell seemed almost too good to be true: prettier in person than on television; a loving daughter, sister, wife, and mother; a devout Christian; an excellent cook; and a generous volunteer for all sorts of worthwhile causes. Fearful that readers wouldn't be able to relate to this superwoman, the writer was relieved when Barbara—apologizing profusely for her "habit"—lit a cigarette and contentedly puffed on it during the interview. *She's human!* thought the interviewer, who mentioned Mandrell's "vice" in the article to show readers that even superwomen have foibles. The *Post* editors, however, deleted the reference to the cigarette because the magazine's publisher doesn't approve of smoking.

Material for an in-depth profile article is usually gathered during a single, lengthy, face-to-face interview (not to exceed two hours) or during several shorter ones. Ideally, the interviewer should have the opportunity not only to ask a wide range of questions, but also to observe the interviewee in various situations, on and off the job. This gives the writer an abundance of resource material: background information that she found at the library, transcripts of the question-and-answer sessions, and pages of interview notes about the subject's personality, appearance, and manner. Secondary interviews with family members, coworkers, and friends add depth and insights.

A profile writer has tremendous power. Depending upon the words chosen to describe the subject, the quotations taken from the interview, and any personal feelings or reactions to the interviewee, a writer can cause readers to like or dislike the person under scrutiny. Even a writer who is determined to be fair in her presentation must make choices, since every word of an interview cannot be included. Selections are made, biases creep in, and impressions are created. (To discover the range of "baggage" that words carry, complete the exercise on the next page.)

Writers need to remember that profiles are not biographies. It's possible to write an interesting and detailed profile without mentioning all of the nuts-and-bolts data about place of birth, education, early jobs, and parents. This kind of boilerplate information is more appropriate for resumés and obituaries. The challenge for the profile writer is to explore thoroughly one or two particularly intriguing or shocking aspects of the interviewee's life.

Profiles are a mainstay of many magazines. Some are short and breezy (500 to 1,000 words); others are long and detailed (several thousand words long). The tone can vary from friendly to formal, depending on the person who is being profiled, the purpose of the piece and the editorial focus of the publication. For example, a business magazine might do a lengthy profile of a corporation's chief executive officer and never mention the man's family, interests, or hobbies. On the other hand, a women's magazine might do a short profile of a celebrity and include intimate items about the star's divorce, battle to lose weight, or substance-abuse problem.

How an author does research for a profile depends completely on the tone and purpose of the piece. In the case of the profile of the corporate CEO, the author would need to acquaint himself with the CEO's company—its history, financial strength, its growth under the CEO's leadership—and prepare a list of questions that would elicit comments from him about the future of the organization. The writer doing a celebrity profile would need to familiarize himself with the star's personal and professional life and create a list of open-ended questions that would encourage the interviewee to respond in an uninhibited and informal manner. (For a sample list of open-ended questions, see page 79.)

Too often beginning writers think that profiles are marketable only if they feature well-known national personalities. Whereas most magazines put pictures of celebrities on their covers, editors also are interested in spotlighting unknown persons who are deserving of publicity. Readers enjoy identifying with people like themselves or a little-known person who has performed a meritorious act or invented a gadget. They are fascinated by celebrities, but they feel comfortable with "real people"—warts and all.

Sending Subtle Signals

These exercises will help you distinguish the shades of difference between words; they also will show you how some words carry "baggage"—they send subtle signals that may be positive or negative.

1. At the left is an adjective that could be used to describe a person. Your task is to select more descriptive words that mean almost the same as the first, but they should vary from positive to negative in the impression they give. See the example.

General Word	Positive	Less Positive	Negative
Old	Mature	Elderly	Decrepit
Overweight	_____	Matronly	_____
Thin	_____	_____	Emaciated
Confident	Assured	_____	_____
Quiet	_____	_____	Aloof
Clever	_____	Sly	_____

2. List several words or short phrases that mean the same, or almost the same, as the word "friend."

_____	_____
_____	_____
_____	_____
_____	_____

Look at your answers and note the different pictures the words paint. A person may be described as serene, private, withdrawn, or snobbish. Each adjective suggests the person is quiet, but is he quiet in a positive or negative way? It all comes down to word choice.

How many synonyms did you list for "friend"? Think about the subtle differences in confidante, colleague, buddy, soul mate, accomplice, crony, sidekick, groupie, pal, partner. Some words suggest deep friendship (soul mate), others a professional relationship (colleague), some have a negative connotation (accomplice).

Newspaper Columns

A newspaper editor we know once commented that most columnists can produce one or two really good columns a year, but few can deliver consistent quality on a regular basis; that is, as many as two, three, or even five columns a week.

One profile writer who has interviewed successful syndicated columnists (Abigail Van Buren, Dr. Joyce Brothers, Art Buchwald, and Erma Bombeck) found that their success stories are the stuff of Hollywood scripts. After reading the advice column published in a San Francisco newspaper, Van Buren marched into the editor's office and said, "I could do better than this!" The editor gave her a stack of letters and told her to draft answers and bring them back at her convenience. She returned within an hour, replies in hand, and "Dear Abby" was born ... or so the story goes. Bombeck, on the other hand, first unleashed her wit on readers of the *Kettering-Oakwood Times,* a suburban weekly newspaper in Ohio. That led to her column for a Dayton daily, and syndication within a year. Her best-selling books and a television comedy show followed.

If writing a nationally syndicated column is your dream, you face a battery of tough critics before the dream can become reality. First, you must convince a newspaper editor—often the editor of your hometown daily—of your column's merit by submitting several sample columns, a list of future topics, and a cover letter that describes the audience you are aiming for, the proposed frequency of the column, and your credentials for writing it. Once over this hurdle—and it is a major one—you can only hope that readers of the newspaper will respond favorably to your work. Usually, an editor will agree to run a column for several weeks and then assess readers' comments.

After you've established a local readership and proven your ability to deliver consistent quality on a regular basis, you (or, better yet, the newspaper editor) can offer the column to a syndicate. To do this you must create a sales packet that includes several of your published columns, a list of future topics, a sampling of supportive letters from readers, your biography, and a list of credits.

If you or the editor succeed in convincing a syndicate to take on your column, consider it a major victory—so far. But you're not there yet. Editors of newspapers across the country have to agree to buy your column from the syndicate and include it in their publications. Finally, readers of the individual newspapers have to respond favorably to the column. Only then will editors *continue* to publish the column.

Aspiring columnists should remember that not all columns are right for a national audience. Although space in most newspapers is tight, an editor of a weekly or regional daily may be receptive to informative and entertain-

Open-Ended Questions

When writing a profile, be sure to ask questions that will reveal the deeper, more whimsical side of an interviewee. Such questions should probe your subject's feelings and opinions rather than prompt a rehash of biographical data that can be found elsewhere.

Review the list of 10 open-ended questions below. Add 10 of your own. Make sure your questions cannot be answered "yes" or "no." Tip: While these questions are recyclable and can be asked in many interviews, use them sparingly and only after you have built a rapport with your interviewee.

1. What, in the last year, has given you the most pleasure?

2. Who or what makes you laugh? Cry?

3. What do you like and dislike most about yourself?

4. Describe for me your idea of a perfect day. With whom would you like to share it?

5. Who are your heroes, living or dead?

6. If you were hospitalized for three months but not too sick, whom (and it can't be a relative) would you want in the next bed?

7. What is your favorite fantasy? (Compete in the luge at the next Olympics? Sing at the Met?)

8. If you were suddenly given a great deal of money and told to spend it on yourself, what would be the first thing you'd buy?

9. What are your favorite three books?

10. What do you know now that you wish you had known at age 18?

11.

12.

13.

14.

15.

16.

17.

18.

19.

20.

ing material with a local angle, but you do need to convince him that your column is different from the other features offered by the newspaper and that you can sustain it month after month. To prove these points, prepare at least five columns (500 to 800 words each) and submit them to the publication's features editor. After a week, follow up with a call.

Although writing a column for a local newspaper won't make you rich (your payment will depend on budget and circulation), there are other benefits. You will get exposure for your byline and will learn how to produce copy under deadline. The editor may ask you to do occasional feature articles that you may be able to recycle to national publications. You'll also build credibility as an expert in your specialty, and this could result in a magazine assignment or even a book contract.

The Final Touches

With periodicals such as *USA Today* making use of four-color photos, bold headlines, multiple insets, and varied type fonts, editors have become more conscious of the visual impact of their publications. Free-lance writers should also consider the eye appeal of the final product. Although the value of a free-lance submission begins with the quality of your copy—*nothing* is more important than your text—eye appeal is also important. If two writers submit manuscripts of comparable quality, the editor may give the nod to the article that visually offers the best packaging possibilities.

Let's look at several enhancements that you can offer an editor to increase your chances of a sale.

Depending on their quality, photographs quickly label a free lancer as either a novice or a professional. Most editors who open an envelope containing both text and pictures will glance first at the photos. If these are poorly composed, technically inferior snapshots, the editor may be prejudiced against the article even before he reads the opening sentence. The pictures may send the negative message: *This writer is a beginner who isn't aware of our publishing standards.*

On the other hand, good photos can work *for* you and heighten an editor's interest in your manuscript. A single representative transparency, 35mm or larger, included with your query letter serves as an indication of the kind of photographs you can provide. If you are sending a completed manuscript, choose an assortment of pictures that best illustrate your words. Don't send original slides, but point out in your cover letter that the enclosed slides are duplicates, and that originals will be forwarded by insured mail upon request.

Photos and transparencies should always be accompanied by captions (also called cutlines). Usually, the publication's art director prepares a page layout, indicates the placement of the photographs, and specifies the character count of the captions. An editor whose responsibilities include writing the captions is grateful to the free lancer who supplies the following information:

- Correctly spelled names and titles of all persons depicted
- An explanation of when and where the picture was taken
- Interesting details that do not restate facts already included in the text
- The name of the photographer who should be credited if the photo is used

Before submitting photographs, request a copy of the publication's photo guidelines. Carefully go through the magazine and note whether the art director's preference is for black-and-white glossies or color transparencies, horizontals or verticals, candids or set-up shots. If you do not take pictures yourself but know a source for good, appropriate photos, pass along the information to the editor.

Hotboxes and sidebars are additional visual elements that can enhance the appearance of magazine pages. Both are offshoots, but not continuations, of the main article. The information contained in a hotbox or sidebar relates to the topic of the parent article but would not necessarily fit well into the flow of the main piece. A sidebar may explore an added dimension or provide a brief detour from the central thrust of the article. A hotbox may magnify a single fact or call attention to an interesting detail not included in the major article. Sidebars usually range in length from 250 words (one column) to 600 words (full page, although this is rare) and often contain a photo or illustration. Hotboxes are limited to about 100 words and do not include artwork.

As an example of how a writer can channel information into an article, sidebar, and hotbox, consider a recently submitted travel manuscript about Seville, Spain. The news peg was Seville's role as host of an international exposition. The main article offered a preview of the major displays that would be included in the exposition. One sidebar featured the Costa del Sol as an attractive side trip for travelers visiting the general area; a second sidebar posed the question, "Will It Rain In Spain?" and predicted weather conditions at this time of year (sizzling hot), and explained how the city planned to use fountains and greenery to cool the public parks. A hotbox told readers "How to Get There from Here" and listed airlines with direct service from the USA.

Information contained in an article, sidebar, and hotbox can often be woven into a single piece. The practice of breaking the elements apart, however, gives readers the option of quickly skimming the shorter components before settling into reading the long article. And, more important, it gives the layout director several elements of various sizes to arrange into an attractive unit. He may choose to put boxes around the sidebars or a light screen over the hotbox. A photo may be dropped into one of the boxes or a quotation taken from the text and blown up into large type for emphasis (this is a "call out"). Whatever format is used, the result will be a visually attractive package to offer readers. Finally, sidebars and hotboxes allow the writer to break out important bits of information that may be different in tone from the main article. A mood piece about a romantic travel destination doesn't have to be compromised by nuts-and-bolts details; an intimate profile of a person doesn't become bogged down with a list of his professional credentials and awards.

Writers can also help break up long columns of text with subheads and bullets. If you are writing a book rather than an article, consider using unifying quotations as lead-ins to the chapters. Other graphic devices are known as "bumper stickers"—catchy phrases most often used in magazines, not books, that summarize key points in your text. They provide the reader with a respite from an overload of information.

In addition to providing visual elements that engage the reader's eye, writers can include participation tactics that will engage the reader's mind. For example, if you're writing a magazine article, consider a sidebar that takes the form of a quiz. The article may explain the relationship between exercise and the relief of stress; but the sidebar will challenge the reader to take a test to determine "How Stressful Is *Your* Life?"

As a writer, you're faced with a constant battle to maintain readers' attention. Boredom is the enemy. The writer who is willing to experiment with innovative techniques to capture and keep reader interest will have a receptive market.

Phase Four:
Selling Your Manuscript

Selling Your Manuscript

"I hate to write, but I love to have written."
—Robert Louis Stevenson

We never have understood what some people mean when they say, "I don't care if I ever get published. I just write for the fun of it."

Fun? What do they mean by fun?

To us, "fun" is not revising a manuscript for the third time because the words don't flow correctly. Is it "fun" to spend two days in the library doing research to verify names, places, and dates, or to write for ten straight hours to meet a revised deadline, or to spend a weekend at home proofreading 250 pages?

Free-lance writing is often lonely and challenging work. The "fun" parts come later: seeing your byline in print and receiving payment from the editor and positive feedback from readers. Without the promise of cash or recognition, it's difficult to stay motivated to write. That's not egotism; that's reality. All writers need to eat, and most like to be recognized for their talent and effort.

With that in mind, let's focus on specific procedures you can use to sell your articles and books.

Handling Rejections

The core strategy in all your marketing efforts will be to provide editors and publishers with exactly the manuscripts they are seeking. Sometimes not knowing what can upset editors and cause them to reject material can work against you. So, let's look at pitfalls to avoid.

Unprofessional appearance

Your manuscript should be typed on paper that is 16 lb. or 20 lb. white bond. Have at least a one-inch margin on the sides, bottom, and top, in proper manuscript format: no rips, smudges, or crossed-out lines or words. The typing should be distinct and dark. (See the facing page for a model manuscript page.)

Wrong publisher

No matter how excellent a manuscript is, it will not be accepted unless it meets the needs of the publisher to whom you submit it. For example, a very entertaining novel would be rejected if submitted to a publisher of college textbooks. A religious publishing house would reject a book on parenting that made no reference to biblical principles, even if the book was well researched. Different publishers have different needs because they are appealing to specific groups of readers.

Shallow research

A book or article must support the claims it makes. Statements and announcements should be supported with references, quotations, and specific research. Remember that writing for publication is different from writing a research paper for a high-school or college English class. Some of your quotations should be gleaned from one-on-one interviews that you have conducted, not just from books and articles written by other authors. Original research always takes priority. No footnotes and endnotes, please!

Inappropriate tone

The "attitude" of the manuscript must match the topic and the publication. You should not give a serious matter light treatment ("The Humorous Side of Hearing Loss") or lecture or preach when you are supposed to be teaching or reporting. Set the correct tone. If you strive for a warm and friendly tone, try using first-or second-person voice ("you," "we," "us"). This is especially effective if you are a member of the audience you are writing for, such as a senior citizen writing for other seniors, or a veteran writing for other vets. For a more formal or professional tone, use third-person voice ("he," "she," "it," "they," "one"). The appropriate tone for a magazine can be easily determined by reading articles in several issues.

Too technical

The manuscript should be written in everyday language (unless it is specifically for a trade journal). Avoid jargon, legalese, and shop talk. Use short sentences, supplemented with examples, anecdotes, and perhaps some sidebars, photos, or charts. Readers should not be burdened with scientific lingo or technical vocabulary they will not understand.

Too biased

Do not present a prejudicial view of a topic unless you are writing an editorial or opinion piece. If articles are obviously pro-union or pro-

[Sample Manuscript Page]

Your Name
Street Address
City, State, Zip
Daytime telephone number

Copyright 19—, Your Name
Approximate word count

How to Prepare a Manuscript

by

Byline Here

Your manuscript should be double-spaced, with each paragraph beginning with an indention. Do not use a print font that is difficult to read (ALL CAPS, *italic,* or ᵈᵉᶜᵒʳᵃᵗⁱᵛᵉ. Research has shown that ragged right type (unjustified) is slightly easier on the eye than justified type (flush margins on both sides). Most editors don't mind if you use a dot-matrix printer, provided the ribbon is new and the impression is dark.

It is not necessary to include a copyright date since the law ensures your ownership of all material you create. Still, many writers—out of habit or fear—type the copyright date. We have indicated the placement of that information if you decide to include it. You need not submit your Social Security number on your manuscript. That information is generally supplied after the manuscript has been accepted and terms negotiated. Remember to number your pages, end the manuscript with the word "end" or with a symbol (###), and secure the pages with a paper clip.

Republican or pro-Swedish or pro any other special-interest group, the feature will be of no use to editors of mass-marketed general-interest publications. (Naturally, editors of in-house or religious denominational periodicals will be the exceptions to this rule since their readerships are special-interest groups.)

Poor timing

You increase the salability of your manuscript if your topic is timely. Unfortunately, timeliness often is out of your control, and luck becomes a factor. For example, in 1990 several editors rejected a well-written article on cults in America. But when the Branch Davidian story from Waco, Texas, burst on the national scene, the topic and the article were suddenly hot—an easy sale for the writer who happened to have the right product at the right time.

The timeliness of some articles is easy to predict. The trick is to submit them precisely when editors need them. Seasonal material must be offered four or six months in advance of holidays or seasonal changes. Christmas features should be marketed to magazines in late spring or early summer. Allow yourself "rejection time," i.e., time to submit your work to a second or third publication if your first marketing attempt isn't successful. (See our "Well-Seasoned Ideas" on the facing page.)

Missing quotations

Articles and chapters without dialogue and quotations are flat, dull, and tedious. Often, articles divided equally between straight narration and quotes will have a lively pace.

Outdated vocabulary

Slang, catch phrases, and clichés may become quickly dated between the time you write an article and when it is submitted, accepted, and finally published. Therefore, you should use standard language for most of your writing.

Weak writing

Spelling, punctuation, grammar, and syntax should be perfect. Don't trust the computer to check your spelling: You need to check it, too. (The computer will allow "reed" when you may have meant "read," since they are both correctly spelled.) Use action verbs and visual nouns. Make the paragraphs short, and link them with smooth transitions. The manuscript should be written informatively and with natural-sounding contractions. Include direct quotations and an obvious "take-away element"—a lesson learned or an insight gained—for the reader.

Well-Seasoned Ideas

Most editors try to include in each issue at least one article tied to the calendar. Avoiding such ho-hum topics as "What Christmas Means to Me" and "The History of Flag Day," try to come up with two or three ideas based on the calendar below. But remember, all editors work from four to six months in advance; take your ideas to market well before they are in season.

January
New Year's Day
Martin Luther King Day
Resolutions
Warm Travel Destinations

February
Valentine's Day
Winter Olympics
Presidents' Day
Leap Year

March
St. Patrick's Day
NCAA Basketball
Mardi Gras
Grammy Awards

April
Tax Deadline
April Fool's Day
Academy Awards
Secretaries' Day

May
Mother's Day
Kentucky Derby
Memorial Day
End of School

June
Weddings
Wimbledon
Summer Gardens
Vacation Time

July
Independence Day
Democratic Convention

August
Back to School
GOP Convention

September
Labor Day
Grandparents' Day

October
Country Music Awards
Halloween
World Poetry Day
Columbus Day

November
Election Day
Veterans Day
Thanksgiving
Education Week

December
Christmas
New Year's Eve
Hanukkah
Kwanzaa

Possibilities: "Five Ways to Thank Your Secretary" (Secretaries' Day); "Military Schools Make Star-Spangled Comeback" (Autumn/back to school); "The Three Most Romantic Restaurants in the Midwest" (Valentine's Day).

Poor topic

The subject of your manuscript should appeal to a large readership of whatever magazine you are submitting it to. No matter how great your writing style, in all likelihood your routine summer vacation won't be of interest to most people.

Avoiding these pitfalls will give you a marketing edge. You also will save yourself and several editors a lot of time and energy.

Studying the Markets

Between 600 and 900 new magazines are launched each year. Although half of them die after a few issues, the others survive and often thrive. This is good news for free lancers, because literally thousands of magazines, newsletters, and journals are eagerly seeking manuscripts. Too often, beginning writers are aware only of the magazines they see each month at their local newsstands. Many other publications are out there waiting to be discovered by free-lance writers.

Several excellent marketing texts can help you discover the names, addresses, phone numbers, editors' names, payment rates, publication frequency, and target audiences of periodicals. We recommend that you begin with *The Writer's Handbook*, edited by Sylvia K. Burack (The Writer, Inc.); *Literary Market Place* (R. R. Bowker Company); *Religious Writers Marketplace*, edited by Sandra H. Brooks and William H. Gentz (Abingdon Press); and *Christian Writers' Market Guide*, edited by Sally E. Stuart (Joy Publishing).

How to begin your survey

Page through these books and study the needs of each magazine. Have a pad handy, and jot down the names of periodicals you might want to contact. Next, write each one a short note asking for a copy of their "Guidelines for Writers," and include a self-addressed, stamped envelope (SASE). Your request will be handled by a secretary or editorial assistant, so don't worry about being clever or creative in your correspondence. You will soon receive (in the envelope you provided) one or more sheets of paper with data about the magazine, its lead time, payment rates, details about its readership, whether it uses cartoons, photos, graphics and other illustrations, which editor to contact for fiction, nonfiction, or poetry, and titles of some of its most recently published articles.

When writing for guidelines, you should also ask for a copy of a recent issue and enclose a check for the cover price of the magazine. (Frequently, editors will send you two or three different copies under separate cover, as long as your check covers the cost of postage.)

Once you've read the guidelines, analyze the magazine. (Consult the checklist on the facing page.) Examine the cover and the coverlines (short

Analyzing a Magazine

Before you contact a magazine editor, use this checklist to analyze the publication.

● <u>Look at the cover</u>
Who or what is featured? To what kind of reader does the subject appeal? Read the coverlines. Who is their target?

● <u>Check the major advertising pages</u>
Look inside the front cover, inside the back cover, at the back cover, and the center spread. What kind of consumer would buy the products promoted on these prominent advertising pages? Are products geared to an age group? income level? gender?

● <u>Turn to the table of contents</u>
Into what sections or departments is the magazine divided? Compare the bylines in the table of contents with the names on the masthead. How many articles have been written by staff members of the magazine? Does that leave much opportunity for free lancers?

● <u>Read the letters to the editor</u>
Can you identify with the people who read this publication? What can you learn about their likes and dislikes that might help you as a contributor to the magazine?

● <u>Study two or three typical articles</u>
What do the guidelines specify as the desired length of articles? Are any short-short features included (contained to one page)? Are articles "continued" in the back of the magazine? Are there any regular columns earmarked for reader submissions (guest editorials, personal stories, contests)? Are articles written in first person or third person? Does any particular category dominate—health, sports, humor?

● <u>Note the photos and illustrations</u>
Are the illustrations color or black-and-white? photos? art? horizontals? verticals? large? small? Check the photo-credit lines. Do writers also submit photos?

phrases on the cover that promote articles inside) to see who is featured and why the editors chose to highlight these subjects. Scan the table of contents and note the departments, topics, and the amount of space given to nonfiction.

Read the letters to the editor. What are people asking about, complaining about, praising, criticizing, and evaluating? Skim two articles. Are they long, short, involved, or succinct?

Now that you have a general feel for the magazine, give it a more in-depth analysis. We suggest the following five steps:

Judge the slant

Although editors do not want material that is biased, no magazine is completely neutral, devoid of a point of view as to the way things should be. The more specialized the magazine, the narrower its editorial scope. Read several articles. What are the perspectives on politics, religion, business, schooling, and family life? Does the magazine lean toward the conservative or liberal view? Is it traditional or progressive in its outlook? If your manuscript can match the magazine's focus, you will increase your odds of being published.

Observe the method of presentation

Each magazine uses specific ways to convey information to its readers. Some use long articles; some use maps and charts; some use cartoons; some use photographs; some use a combination of all of these options. Examine the magazine carefully and then submit articles in a format that best matches the magazine's format.

Note the variety

Some magazines want a very limited range of material; for example, *The American Legion Magazine* looks only for articles of interest to veterans. Other periodicals, such as inflight magazines, cover from 20 to 30 different topics each month. Note also the variety of writing styles. You may discover that a single magazine provides opportunities for several different kinds of your manuscripts.

Balance

Determine how much of the magazine is devoted to each major topic of interest. For example, if a magazine is targeted to homemakers and its four major areas of concentration are crafts, cooking, child care, and sewing, count the number of pages of articles and ads related to each topic area. If 25 of a magazine's 100 pages contain information about crafts, then your article about crafts will have a 25% chance of finding a home there. However, if only 10 pages are devoted to crafts, the odds are nine to one against your selling your article to that periodical. Seek a magazine in which the emphasis on crafts is higher.

Evaluate the levels of comprehensiveness

How in-depth are the reporting and writing in the magazine? Do articles present just an overview of subjects, or do they analyze them in great detail? You will have to adjust your articles to correspond in depth and research to whatever this magazine usually publishes.

Having followed the procedure of seeking a market, procuring the writers guidelines and sample copies of the magazine, and then analyzing the magazine, you will next be ready to contact an editor there by sending a query letter.

Writing Query Letters

A query letter presents an idea for an article to a magazine editor. As we mentioned earlier, it is not wise to write your article first and then try to sell it. The editor may like your idea, but may want a slightly different slant or perhaps 250 fewer words than you had planned. Get the go-ahead and specific instruction, *then* write the article.

Some editors, particularly travel editors, will consider "multiple pitches." Say you are planning a trip to Great Britain and your itinerary includes several stops that could result in a variety of articles. You begin your query letter with a sentence or two of introduction, then quickly capsulize three article possibilities in a "bullet" format:

- Located at the site of England's first coffee house, the Frank Cooper Marmalade Museum in Oxford traces the popularity of a British tradition. Marmalade is the spread of choice in the U.K. (it accounts for 60 percent of sweet-spread sales), and this landmark features old catalogues, posters, ledger books, and a retail shop. I envision a short feature of about 750 words with color photos.

- Before you leave the Tower of London, stop by and say cheerio to the royal ravens. There are six (one is named Ronald Raven), and legend claims the Tower will collapse if the ravens ever fly the coop. An interview with the ravenmaster will detail colorful bird lore and trivia. My article could be about the jewels with a sidebar on the ravens, or about the ravens with a sidebar on the jewels. Your choice.

- Dying for a cuppa? Every man, woman, and child over 10 in the U.K. drinks about four cups of tea a day. Whether you take high tea at the Ritz or a spot of Earl Grey at a local lunch counter, when in England, do as the English do. This travel/food feature will include a sidebar of recipes for scones, mille-feuilles and strawberry tarts.

The editor will skim your list and determine if she wants you to pursue any of the ideas. She may even suggest a few ideas of her own. For example, she may suggest that the feature on tea be accompanied by a sidebar on the marmalade museum. If she's not familiar with your work, she may ask to see a few clips of previous work or ask you to submit the article on speculation.

Make your query letter as specific as possible in describing the contents of your proposed article. Even if you haven't done a great deal of research, give the editor an idea of what questions your article will answer. The mapping exercise on the facing page will help you with this. Condense your idea to a few words, and write the words in the center of a sheet of paper. Create offshoots of the idea as subtopics that you might explore in your article. Be a name dropper, and mention one or two sources you plan to interview as part of your research.

Always make sure your article is appropriate for the magazine you are contacting. "Ten Ways to Make Spicy Giblet Gravy for Thanksgiving" might be perfect for the November issue of *Family Circle* but not for *Weight Watchers Magazine.* True, both magazines discuss food at length, but from very different viewpoints.

Be unique in what you offer. Study back issues of the magazine so that you won't suggest a subject covered in a recent issue.

Don't be dull. Too many writers think, "Oh, it's just a query letter. My article will be much more interesting." If an editor reads a dull, plodding query letter, what do you suppose he will assume your article is going to be? You should consider your query a sales letter. (It is!) Make it captivating. Some writers like to use the lead they have planned for their article as the lead for their query letter. This gives them a running start on the article and grabs the editor's attention.

Make sure your grammar is correct, your spelling perfect (including the hyphenations at the end of lines), and your typing clear and clean. Estimate how long your article will be, based on the word-length limitations specified in the writers guidelines you received, explain the availability of photos and graphics, and offer a projected completion date.

You might want to highlight any publication credits and background items that apply specifically to the article you're proposing to write. For example, if your article is about "The Pros and Cons of Home Schooling," it would be perfectly appropriate to note that you are a former teacher who home schooled two of your four children. However, if you are a florist, there's no need to mention your profession, since it has no bearing on your research or your credibility. It is also appropriate to mention briefly, in a separate paragraph, other publication credits.

In closing the letter, don't add such statements as "I'm a loyal subscriber to your magazine, and I love every issue." Make sure that your phone num-

Queries: Mind Mapping

Your query letter should give an editor a quick overview of your article's contents. More than merely suggesting a topic, you need to highlight various aspects of the topic that your article will explore. To help you determine all the directions your article might take, try this mapping exercise. Write your general topic in the center of the page, and then brainstorm all the spinoff possibilities or points you want the finished article to cover. After you have exhausted your ideas, number the subtopics according to their importance.

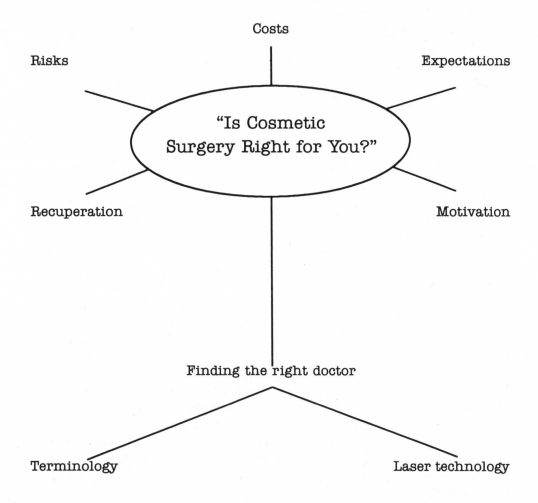

ber and return address are on the top of the page. Remember to include an SASE. If your query is about doing a profile interview with an interesting person, you might also want to mention that you have secured photo release forms (page 121) and, if needed, publication consent agreements (page 119).

Address your query letter to a person by name, not simply a title, such as "Managing Editor" or "Travel Editor," so your letter will arrive on the correct person's desk much faster. Your market guidebooks, the publication's guidelines for writers, or—most reliable of all—the masthead of the magazine will tell you the names of the magazine's editors.

If you receive no reply in four weeks, send a follow-up postcard asking about the status of your query letter. If you receive no reply to the postcard, try another publication.

Above all, be professional in every piece of correspondence you send to an editor. One magazine editor who reads countless query letters from free lancers says writers try too hard to be creative. Among gimmicks you should never use: an article proposal composed of words snipped from newspaper like a ransom note; a manuscript slipped into a plain brown wrapper sprayed gold to grab attention (still sticky when it arrived); a generous sample of Fort Lauderdale's white sand to "sell" an article about that city's beaches; a query letter that arrived with two pages glued together. (The author was convinced that editors never read his often-rejected manuscripts. He thought if his submission was returned with the pages still stuck, his theory would be proven correct.)

Writers often ask whether it's a good idea to send simultaneous query letters to several different magazines proposing the same idea. There's danger in that approach: If two competing magazines want your ideas, you will have to disappoint one, which may strain relations in the future. Instead, sending several query letters to different magazines about different article ideas will boost the odds of your getting an assignment, and you won't disappoint any editors.

Preparing Book Proposals

Forget the rumors. Here is a fact: Book publishers *do* read book proposals. What's more, many unknown writers do get contracts, thanks to well-written proposals. Because the elements that combine to make a well-written proposal seldom vary, let's take a moment to review them.

Your first step is to come up with an interesting subject with strong commercial sales possibilities. Keep in mind that while publishers serve the public by providing entertaining and informative material, they also *must* make a profit. Quite often, the choice of subject matter alone can be the selling factor for a book; so, choose carefully.

Topics have a life span, and it's up to every writer to know if an idea is on the upswing or has already peaked. For example, in the area of business books, the hot topic in the '60s was time management; in the '70s it switched to enhancing customer loyalty; in the '80s it shifted to downsizing office and physical plant operations; and in the '90s it is focused on retaining key personnel. Interest in each of these topics has never died and never will as long as new ways of studying them are developed. However, readers are always eager for completely new subjects.

Where can you find ideas for new books? Go to the reference section of the library and skim the titles in current editions of *Books in Print, Forthcoming Books, 80 Years of Best Sellers,* and *Subject Guide to Books in Print* (all R.R. Bowker Co.). If you already have an idea for a book, you can find out whether or not it has previously been published—and when. Perhaps you will be able to put a new spin on the topic, or maybe the previous books are now dated or out of print and you have current information that hasn't been published in book form.

If you do not have an idea for a book yet, scanning titles and reading summaries of their contents may stimulate your thoughts. Make notes. Consider how you might write a companion book, a book presenting a counter-viewpoint, or a supportive work of something already published. An overlooked topic could provide an opportunity for you, especially if you have a new angle.

Read contemporary magazines for timely articles on an unusual subject. Our book, *How to Stop Living for the Applause: Help for Women Who Need to Be Perfect,* grew out of a published magazine article about the struggles of balancing a full-time writing career with family obligations. An editor read the article and asked us if we thought it could be expanded into a book. We submitted a book proposal, and a contract was signed.

Once you've come up with what you feel is a good topic for a book, you need to test the idea's merit. Work through the "Planning Your Nonfiction Book" exercise on page 99. Be as specific as you can in answering questions about the timeliness of the topic, the competition in the marketplace, and the research you will conduct to produce the book. Consult references such as *The Writer's Handbook* and *Literary Market Place* to identify at least three potential publishers. Check research indexes at the library for possible competition, as well as *Publishers Weekly* for forthcoming titles.

If your book falls into a specific category, such as a cookbook or a children's picture book, concentrate first on approaching publishing companies that specialize in these types of books. Eliminate from your list any houses that note that they deal only with literary agents. (You may later decide to use the services of an agent, but let's assume you intend to market your book on your own.)

As for sending book proposals to several publishers simultaneously, most publishers do not consider this a good idea. The reasons are similar to those for article queries, discussed earlier. If two publishers express interest, you are in the awkward position of making a choice and explaining your decision to the "rejected" publisher. It's not the way to get ahead in this business. (Agents can get away with that, as well as with multiple submissions of completed manuscripts, because editors know that is how they operate. It is not recommended for writers.)

Instead of circulating six copies of the proposal for your cookbook, prepare three different proposals on three different topics: perhaps one on career planning for non-college graduates, one on organic gardening, and the one on cooking. Send each to a different publisher. Whichever one comes back with an acceptance will be the one you will write.

The proposal itself has five standard components: (1) the cover letter; (2) the synopsis; (3) the table of contents; (4) the outline or annotated table of contents; and (5) two or three sample chapters.

The cover letter

The cover letter should be like a carnival-barker's pitch: It must really sell your book idea. Don't be coy or reserved. Be excited, specific, optimistic, purposeful. Stress the fact that your approach to this topic is new and that even when dealing with established ideas, you will support them with new statistics, examples, sources, views, experiences, and insights.

Here is some of the information that needs to be included in a good cover letter: the estimated length (in pages or word count) the book will be when completed; how much time you will need to complete the book; your credentials for writing this book (job experiences and formal education if relevant, previous writing credits, your personal interest in the topic); your projected markets for the book (colleges? libraries? book clubs? lecture tours? bookstores? readers' groups? collectors?); and your ability to promote the book on radio, TV, at readings, in clubs, at conventions, and through the print media. Unlike a succinct query letter (one page), the cover letter may be from two to four pages long. See page 101 for an example.

The synopsis

You next need to prepare a synopsis, usually about 1,000 words long. It should have the excitement of a dust jacket blurb, along with the detail of a book review in *The New York Times*. Explain what the book will cover, what its format will be, what new insights will be presented, and what will make it worth the reader's time.

Table of contents

Next, type a one-page table of contents. Editors like to see this for several reasons. It will suggest a possible layout for the book—whether or not you

Planning Your Nonfiction Book

Before embarking on a book-length manuscript, sketch out a blueprint for its construction. This will help you decide if your book is marketable and will be of value when you create the book proposal to send to agents, editors, and publishers. Answer these 12 questions as completely as you can.

1. I want to write a book about _____
_____.

2. The audience for this book is _____.

3. My working title is _____.

4. I envision the book to be about ____ pages and ____ chapters.

5. This book is timely right now because _____
_____.

6. I am qualified to write this book because _____
_____.

7. Other books written about this topic are _____
_____.

8. My book is different from (or better than) the others because
_____.

9. Persons I will need to contact/interview for my book include
_____.

10. Other research I must do includes (stats, questionnaires, background reading, etc.) _____
_____.

11. Illustrations might be _____
_____.

12. Three publishers that might be interested in the book are ____
_____.

plan to include an introduction, separate sections, units or chapters, end-notes, an appendix, a glossary, an index, photo inserts, and an epilogue. This will help the editor visualize the extent of technical work needed on the book.

The outline

The simplest and most functional way to approach making an outline is to type the title of the book at the top of the page, with your byline under it, and then the title of each chapter (Chapter One: The Marriage Ceremony). Follow that with a succinct one-paragraph summary of what will be covered in that chapter—for example, the key facts you will focus on and an explanation of how they will be presented. These chapters will indicate how you plan to sustain readers' interest and make the transitions from one chapter to another.

These brief chapter summaries should also mention whether the chapter will contain sidebars, graphics, or photographs.

Sample chapters

Finally, you will need to send along two or three completed chapters. Most writers send chapters one and two because they are writing their book chronologically, but this isn't mandatory. Since the editor has read your synopsis and outline, she already has an overview of the book's content; now she needs to know if you can write the book. The sample chapters will answer that question.

Include an SASE with your submission in case your proposal is rejected. Don't be overly discouraged by rejection. The return of a proposal merely means that *one* editor at *one* publishing house on *one* day didn't like *one* idea. It doesn't necessarily mean that your book isn't publishable or that you aren't a good writer.

Good books are rejected for a lot of reasons. Sometimes the publisher has just paid a huge advance for another book and the company is temporarily short of cash. Another book similar to yours may have already come in and the editor has closed a deal for it.

Rejection can also occur because an editor misjudges your book's market-ability. For instance, Wayne Dyer's *Your Erroneous Zones* was rejected several times before it was accepted, and it became a best seller, proving that editors aren't infallible in their judgments. There are dozens of similar examples.

If your proposal has made the rounds of five or six publishers and has been rejected, you should examine your concept and your proposal again. Ask someone whose opinion you trust to critique it for you. Take it to a writers' conference and submit it to a visiting agent or editor for evaluation. If editors who have rejected your proposal have sent you letters explaining

[Sample Cover Letter for a Book Proposal]

Date

Name, Address

Dear Mr. _____:

We are an impatient society. Years ago people waited five days for a stagecoach to arrive; today, we're upset if we miss one section of a revolving door going into a bank. A decade ago a "fast" response to someone's letter was something sent by overnight mail; today, people want replies by fax or e-mail within seconds of sending an initial message.

Time is of the essence in all we do. Yet, no matter how many technological gadgets we develop, we cannot put more hours into the day. What we *can* do, however, is make better use of the hours we have.

My new book, *Staying Ahead of Time,* will show how this can be done. The 50,000-word manuscript will be slivered into 30 short chapters, each containing an explanation of a specific procedure for managing time more effectively. Why so many chapters? I've discovered that people are so pressured today, they don't have time to study time management. By making the chapters compact, I enable the reader to complete a segment while riding the subway to work or sitting atop an exercise bike. Just 10 minutes a day for one month will complete the book and provide the reader with a range of new tools to master time.

Two years ago I wrote a three-part series for *Sales Builder* magazine on contemporary approaches to time management. Reader response was so positive, the senior editor of the magazine asked me to do a monthly column. Since then, I've written about numerous aspects of time management, ranging from setting goals to running effective meetings. I now want to develop my columns into chapters. Enclosed are three sample chapters, a table of contents, an outline, and a synopsis. I can deliver a completed manuscript within 90 days of signing a contract.

Besides being a columnist for *Sales Builder,* I am a contributor to magazines such as *Marketing Digest, Self-Employer News,* and *Today's Executive.* The editors of these periodicals assure me that they will review my book and provide endorsement quotations for the dust jacket. I also teach seminars on time management at colleges, corporations, and small businesses, where I can direct-market the book to students.

If you feel that my manuscript would be something you would be interested in publishing, you can contact me by phone, fax, or e-mail. I look forward to your response.

Sincerely,

why your idea was rejected, give careful thought to their points of criticism and use them as guides for revising your proposal.

If your proposal is not rejected and an editor becomes interested in your book idea, he will respond in one of three ways:

1. By offering you a contract
2. By asking to see more sample chapters before making a decision
3. By discussing with you ideas for taking your original concept in a different direction: changing the intended readership, perhaps, or changing the format of your table of contents.

It is then up to you to sign the contract or negotiate the terms of the document, provide the additional chapters, or agree or refuse to change the content of your book.

Some publishers ask for a completed book manuscript when dealing with previously unpublished writers. You can handle this situation in one of several ways. If you feel that writing an entire nonfiction book would be a good learning experience for you and would allow you to write at your own pace (without the pressure of a deadline), then by all means write the book. However, if you don't feel that writing an entire book is a fair demand, since it means you may not have enough income to live on and you also might have to do major rewrites if the publisher doesn't like the finished work, then simply submit your proposal to other publishers. Play by your rules, not theirs. You might try approaching a literary agent to represent you, since they almost always like to work with proposals in securing book contracts. Agents usually prefer to represent established authors, but there are some who do take on first-time writers.

Contracts—Closing the Deal

Most first-time authors are so delighted to have a publisher accept their manuscript for publication, they never dream of arguing any points in the "standard" contract offered to them. And, actually, most beginning authors do not have a record of strong sales from previous books to justify their asking for special considerations from publishers. Nevertheless, signing a book contract is a business deal and it should be approached with as much business savvy as possible.

We suggest that if you have any questions about the fairness or legality of a book contract, you seek the counsel of an attorney with experience in this area of the law or, when you get a contract, let the attorney handle it.

Publishers are a lot like bankers. They are in business to make as much profit as possible. Even though without writers like you neither the publisher nor the banker could succeed, they sometimes try to make you think that without them, *you* couldn't succeed. That's not true.

We have found that the key to negotiating changes in a standard contract is to explain why you feel the change would be beneficial to both sides. For example, most standard book contracts call for the publisher and the author to share equally in any money that is earned by selling excerpts ("second rights") from the book to magazines. However, in signing one of our contracts recently, we asked that the clause be rewritten to give all excerpt earnings to the authors.

Our publisher asked why we felt we needed to receive all the income from excerpts. We explained that we knew the publisher did not have the personnel available to spend many weeks lining up excerpt sales for our book, yet we were willing to do this, and we felt we deserved whatever we could earn from the effort. We also pointed out that excerpts in magazines would increase interest in the book and, thus, increase sales. This appealed to the publisher and seemed beneficial to both sides. So, the contract was changed in our favor on that point.

If you have never negotiated a contract, here are a few areas you can consider discussing with your publisher:

• Unless the manuscript is a "work made for hire" agreement (a flat payment assignment), ask to have the work copyrighted in your name rather than in the name of the publisher.

• You might consider adding a clause to the contract noting that the publisher will at least consult the author in regard to the design of the book's jacket.

• The "Discontinuance of Publication" clause generally specifies that if the book goes out of print (usually determined by fewer than 300 sales per year), the author will be allowed to ask the publisher that all publication rights revert to the author. The publisher will then have 30 days to respond to the letter or six months to reissue the book; otherwise, publication rights will return to the author.

• A "Bankruptcy" clause should explain that if the publisher goes into bankruptcy, insolvency, reorganization or dissolution, the publisher's rights to the author's book shall terminate.

• An "Examination of Books of Accounts" should state that the author has the right (at his or her own expense) to examine the publisher's books in so far as they relate to the sales of the author's books. A more gracious way of approaching this would be to submit a "Royalty Assessment Statement" questionnaire (see page 105) asking the publisher to explain how earnings, expenses, and royalties were determined.

• The matter of royalty payment frequency is a sore point with many authors. If the author is paid just once a year, the publishers get to keep the author's royalties in their bank account, thus earning interest off the author's money. That is why some writers ask for either larger advances or royalty payments every 90 days. However, some of the smaller publishers may be unable to accommodate these requests, in which case we suggest you yield on this issue in exchange for the publisher giving in on a different point of contract disagreement.

• If there is anything even remotely controversial in your book, you should try to get it in writing that the publisher will cover your liability against litigation in the publisher's own umbrella insurance coverage. Even then, the deductible on such policies can run as high as $50,000, so you won't be provided free coverage. Still, some libel and invasion of privacy lawsuits filed against authors and publishers have run into the millions of dollars; so, it is best to get whatever coverage is available.

• Sometimes publishers sit on a completed manuscript after having received it from the author. The author expects the book to be printed and released in short order, but the publisher may want to devote time to other projects. To protect against this, an "Acceptability of Manuscript" clause might be worded something on this order:

> Publisher shall notify author within sixty (60) days of receipt of a manuscript as to its acceptability or nonacceptability. If in the sole opinion of the publisher the work is unacceptable to the publisher, the publisher shall provide the author with a detailed list of reasonably required changes, and the author shall have sixty (60) days from the receipt of said list to make such changes. If in the sole opinion of the publisher the revised work is unacceptable to the publisher, he may reject it by written notice within sixty (60) days of delivery of the revised manuscript.

• Finally, the elements of "Subsidiary Rights Licenses" should be spelled out as specifically as possible. Such licenses could include product endorsements, T-shirts, book clubs, paperback editions, movies, video games, computer software, book markers, posters, audiotapes, toys, TV specials, or radio dramas.

Famed editor Maxwell Perkins once said, "The book belongs to the author." Before turning your creative work over to a publisher, elements of mutual gratification must be agreed on—not dictated by one party or the other. Most publishers are eager to establish long-lasting relationships with their writers. Authors usually have the same goal. How contracts are handled will often make or break that relationship.

Understanding Royalties

We have talked to many new writers who were stunned by their first book royalty payments. A few of these writers were pleasantly surprised because they never expected their books to sell as well as they did. Most others, however, were shocked at how low the earnings were.

There are several reasons royalty statements may show earnings different from what the author expected.

[Sample Royalty Assessment Statement]

Dear Publisher,

I am in receipt of your recent royalty statement for _____ by
_____. Please supply me with the following informa-
tion omitted in your statement and provide for it in future
accountings:

_____ accounting period covered by the statement

_____ initial publication date

_____ first and subsequent size of printings

SALES THIS PERIOD

	Royalty Rate	Royalty Base	Copies Sold	Copies Returned	Net Copies	Royalty Earned
____ Regular	%	$				$
____ Wholesale						
____ % Discount						
____ Mail order						
____ Special						
____ Remaindered						
____ % Discount						

OTHER EARNINGS (reprints, book clubs, serial, foreign, other)

Units	Rate	Amount	Author's Share
			% $
____ (source)			
____ Copy of licensee's statement			
____ Total copies sold last period			
____ Total copies sold this period			
____ Total copies sold to date			

____ Deductions properly itemized (advances, unearned balance,
book purchases, etc.) with attached statement, where
applicable

____ % held as reserve against returns

The amount for which the publisher sells the books is a key factor. For example, if a publisher sells 3,000 copies of a $20 book at a wholesale price of $12, the company earns $36,000. However, some publishers skip the middle party (bookstore) and sell directly to readers via catalogs or direct mail. So, if the company sells the same 3,000 books, 1,000 at retail ($20,000) and 2,000 at wholesale ($24,000), the company's total earnings rise to $44,000. If the author's contract stipulated that she was to receive a percentage of the book's total earnings, then she would receive more money than she had expected.

However, it also works the opposite way. Some publishers will sell their books at less than wholesale ("quantity" or "special discount") in order to encourage bookstores to place larger orders. Thus, if 2,000 books are sold at wholesale ($12 each) and 1,000 at a special discount ($9 each), the company will earn only $33,000. In turn, the author's royalties will decrease.

Overseas sales are also a mixed blessing. If a book is sold to a foreign publisher who plans to translate it into another language, this helps make the author internationally famous and it brings in additional earnings. However, literary agents take an extra 10% to 15% of the author's royalty earnings for overseas sales. Also, translator's fees are sometimes divided between the foreign publisher and the author. And, even worse, many U.S. publishers have a clause in their book contracts that stipulates that authors and their U.S. publishers will receive equal earnings on all overseas sales. So, if the agent gets 20% and the translator gets 10% and the U.S. publisher gets half of the remaining 70%, the author will receive only 35% of her regular *wholesale* royalty earnings.

Book club sales have their down side, too. If a book club actually buys books from the publisher for resale to its members, the author benefits greatly. Regretfully, it seldom works out that way. Almost always, book clubs will merely buy or rent the book publisher's "plates" (camera-ready layouts, cover designs, and page negatives). The book clubs will then run off their own versions of the book, usually with poorer quality paper and flimsy covers, and will sell thousands of copies at a very low price to their club members. Publishers are willing to cooperate in this because they believe it will give the book "high visibility" and thus promote the author's career and enhance future book sales.

Another determinant of earnings is called the "reserve against returns." Most publishers will not send all of an author's royalty earnings to him or her, even though the money has been received from the bookstores, libraries and other customers, because if the bookstores are not able to sell all of the author's books, they will ship them back to the publisher and ask for a refund (or a credit). As such, if 10,000 copies of a book were ordered and paid for and sold, the author would earn royalties on 10,000 books. However, if only 7,000 books were sold and 3,000 were returned for refunds, the author would earn royalties on only 7,000 books. So, to protect themselves from overpaying authors for books that might be returned, publishers hold back some of the royalty earnings until they are certain the books really have sold and won't be returned.

Authors sometimes become outraged if they feel this procedure is being abused. For instance, if the publisher pays royalties only once per year and holds back $10,000 of a writer's royalties as a reserve against returns, that means the publisher can keep that money in the bank and earn interest on it. This is why many established authors insist that their book contracts stipulate that only 5% of royalty earnings can be held in reserve, and even then, for no more than six months.

A final factor is the selling off of inventory when a book goes out of print. If a book usually sells at wholesale for $10 and at special discount for $7, the price may fall even lower when it is remaindered. By this time, all of the primary and secondary markets for the book have been saturated and the publisher just wants to get rid of the remaining stock. A discount catalogue house or company may be willing to buy all remaining copies, but at only $2 each, making the author's earnings extremely low. (For this reason, authors sometimes like to buy up all the remaindered copies of their own books from their publishers. They then sell them a few books at a time at full retail price when they go on lecture tours or appear at conventions or business conferences.)

If you have doubts about the accuracy of your royalty statement, you can submit the "Royalty Assessment Statement" to your publisher or you can discuss the matter with your publisher's accounting department or your literary agent.

Keeping Financial Records

As a writer, you need to remember that *documentation* is the key word when dealing with the Internal Revenue Service. If you are going to deduct something as a legitimate business expense, you are going to have to prove you spent the money and that, even though you are working part-time, you are writing professionally. So, rule number one in regard to keeping financial records is "pay by check or get a receipt."

What expenses are considered legitimate for a free-lance writer? Actually, there are many. Among them:

Consultation expenses can be deducted if you hire a free-lance editor to proofread and edit your manuscript before you submit it to a publisher. Likewise, the tax preparation fee your accountant charges you is deductible. You can also deduct the fee an attorney charges you to review your book contract or the fee a literary agent charges you to sell your manuscript.

Subscriptions to writers' magazines, newsletters, trade journals and writing annuals as well as professionally related books are deductible. And, don't forget to include membership fees charged by information services and usage fees that are linked to online research.

Business-related phone calls to your editors, publishers, coauthors, literary agent, and people you use as interview sources for articles or books are all deductible. This is also true of fax messages and electronic mail sent to these people. Keep a record of everyone you call, when, why, the results of the call, and the cost.

Supplies such as paper, printer cartridges, pencils, pens, business letterhead stationery, envelopes, notepads, cassette tapes, floppy disks, film, ribbons, paper clips, staples, tape, and other items needed to maintain a writing career are deductible expenses.

All *postage costs* related to mailing query letters, manuscripts, and business invoices may be deducted.

A *safe-deposit box rental fee* may be deducted if the box is used to store materials related to your career, such as valuable interview tapes, original manuscripts in hard copy form or on disk, book contracts or rare photographs. If you use half the box for personal items (deeds, bonds, jewelry) and half for your writing materials, only half of the rental fee can be deducted.

Equipment and furnishings related to a career in writing, such as a word processor, fax machine, electric pencil sharpener, camera, writing desk, photocopier, cassette tape recorder, computer and printer, and filing cabinets usually qualify for either tax write-offs or investment credits. Sometimes your accountant will amortize the cost of big-ticket items over three to five years.

Business mileage deductions are based on a per-mile rate which varies from year to year with the IRS (check with your accountant on this). Automobile trips to interviews, writer's conferences, meetings with editors or agents, talk show appearances or autograph parties should be recorded by date, destination, and beginning and ending odometer readings.

Tuition for self-improvement courses that enhance your writing career can be deducted. These include writers' conferences, writing workshops and seminars, and correspondence courses.

The cost of a *passport* is deductible if you travel for book research or as a travel writer for a newspaper or magazine.

If you maintain a *home office* that is used strictly for your writing career and you maintain no other office (such as a college teacher's office), you may deduct that part of your rent or mortgage payment from your taxes. For example, if you have nine rooms in your home and one is an office, you may deduct one-ninth of your rent or mortgage payments as a business expense. The same applies to your heating and electricity bills. Be aware that if you set up shop at your dining-room table a couple of times a week, your dining room does *not* qualify as an office.

For the record

You will need to maintain two sets of business books. The first will be a "cash receipts journal." This will be a record of all of your writing-related earnings (royalties, advances, expense allowances, work-for-hire paychecks). Your setup should include columns for the date the payment arrived, the payor (magazine's name or book publisher), the check number, the amount, and a running total. As an example:

Cash Receipts Journal

Date	Payor	Check Number	Amount	Running Total
1/27	*City Gazette*	#66229	$ 50	$ 50
2/09	*Ladies' Day*	#119866	$175	$225
2/14	*New Times*	#442	$400	$625

You will also need a "cash disbursements journal." It will serve as a record of all your writing-related expenses. The ledger should have columns for the date the expense was incurred, the receiver of the payment, your check number (or receipt record), the amount paid out, the item purchased, and a running total of the year's expenses.

Cash Disbursements Journal

Date	Receiver	Check Number	Item	Amount	Running Total
1/06	Supply Shop	#763	Fax paper	$18.72	$18.72
1/11	Comp. Corner	#821	Disks	$29.58	$48.30

Be sure to have a qualified accountant assist you in your tax work each year. You can help your own cause a great deal, however, by starting now to keep account records.

Cyclical Marketing

If you were to examine the back issues of the nation's leading magazines, you would discover that they have been covering the same topics over and over at regular intervals. True, the titles are different and so are the authors, but seldom the subjects.

The reason editors repeat articles on subjects previously covered is not just to update available information. It is also because audiences change. One year a young woman might subscribe to *Seventeen;* three years later, however, she'll switch to *Modern Bride;* two years later, she will be reading *Self;* and a few years beyond that, she'll be scanning *Family Circle.* For a time a boy will read *Boy's Life,* then switch to *Hot Rod,* then *Campus Life,* and eventually end up with a subscription to *Field and Stream* or *GQ.* As each magazine's audience changes, the editors must focus again on article topics for their current audience.

As a free lancer, you will find this to be important marketing knowledge. By studying back issues of a magazine that you wish to break into and thereby discovering repetitive themes, you can project what its future rotational needs will be. (See facing page.) Let's assume that there is a magazine called *Big-Time Investments* that pays 35¢ a word for articles. You want to make a sale there, so you go to the library and read the bound volumes or microfilm of its issues for the past three to five years.

As you begin to read the article titles in the table of contents, you make a note of the broad topics they cover. Each time an issue runs an article about one of these topics, you make a check mark on your list, noting the date it appeared. (Of course, if this material is in a database that you can access, your job will be easier.)

At the end of your examination, your checklist may reveal that *Big-Time Investments* has run an article about diamonds every two years, an article about gold every 18 months, an article about silver annually, an article about mutual funds every six months, and an article on real estate every other issue. You've discovered the hottest general topic for this magazine: real estate.

Next, you make a list of eight or 10 of the article titles that relate to real-estate investments and discover that three of them are "Buying Condos with No Downpayment"; "Full Financing for Rental Properties"; and "No Up-Front Cash for Eastern Land Tracts." This tells you that the specific article topic that readers look for most frequently is how to invest in real estate with no initial investment capital.

Knowing this, you next read all articles that *Big-Time Investments* has published on that topic during the past several years, taking detailed notes. It isn't hard. You've found a dozen different articles on the topic, but after you've read four of them, they've started to repeat a lot of the basic information.

Having analyzed your notes for this basic material, you will want to find some sort of new angle for covering it again. There are a variety of ways to go about this. You can procure quotations from experts in the field who have not as yet been featured in this magazine. You can develop unique sidebars. You can provide different photographs or specialized computer graphics that will give a "face lift" to this topic's artistic layout. You can and should also include anything previously unpublished about the topic, such

Dependable Magazine Topics that Appear Regularly

In the list below, you will find categories of many cyclical article features. Read them and note how familiar they are to you. After reviewing the list, see how the pattern of discovery works. Get a stack of magazines and see if you can find cyclical articles that fit into a standard topic. Write them down.

Category	Specific article topics within category
Food:	Recipes, cake designing, specialty desserts
Health:	Diets, exercise programs, vitamins, sleep
Love:	Dating, marriage, sex, divorce, widowhood
Family:	Pregnancy, childbirth, adoption, the elderly
Career:	College, job interviews, salary negotiations
Money:	Investments, savings, taxes, estate planning
Politics:	Candidates, laws, lobbies, investigations
Religion:	Cults, sects, media outreach, prophecy
Entertainment:	Travel, hobbies, athletics, music
Fashion:	Trends, colors, fabrics, designs, costs

Now, it's your turn:

Sports:

Education:

Electronics:

Medicine:

Cooking:

Writing:

Art:

Hobbies:

Teaching:

Humor:

as new laws and regulations, current research and studies, and/or recently reported case histories.

When you submit your feature, the editor will recognize it as exactly the material her readers want. When she purchases it from you, she may also enclose a letter asking, "Have you ever written anything about mutual funds?"

Naturally, you will be only too eager to go back and discover what kind of mutual funds article has been most popular in *Big-Time Investments* during the previous five years. After having discovered it, you will prepare a new version of it, submit it, and once again please the editor.

Keep your original real estate article (as published) handy. A year later you can do a new version of that article, only you won't have to expend as much energy assembling the standard information. You'll already have it at hand.

Resale of Manuscripts

After investing a lot of time and effort in producing an article, the smart writer tries to wring as much profit out of the same project as possible. Some free lancers won't write a feature unless they foresee four sales in it. And that's a *minimum*. An interview with actor James Dean's dance teacher was parlayed into seven free-lance sales; a piece about the inventor of a three-wheeled car has been published in 23 magazines. A first-person account of a two-week trek into the jungle of Belize appeared in publications as diverse as *CompuServe Magazine* and *The Christian Reader;* an article about body language was published in *Indianapolis Woman, Today's Christian Woman,* and was incorporated in a book titled *The Workplace.*

Multiple marketing is legal, ethical, and lucrative, and it can be practiced in two ways. You can sell the same article time and time again without changing a word, or you can create several different articles based on the same research. If you make no changes or only minor alterations in a manuscript that has been sold previously, you offer "reprint rights" to subsequent editors. If you choose a new slant, a different lead, and incorporate fresh quotations from your interviewees, you may offer "first rights" because the manuscript is virtually a new property. Most editors do not mind this as long as previous appearances of the article have not reached their specific readers.

As you consider recycling your articles for multiple sales, keep these four points in mind:

● *Not every article has the potential to be sold more than once.*

Some material may be *too dated* and may become obsolete before you can sell it again. For example, an article on "The Year of the American Craft," assigned by *The Saturday Evening Post,* was marketable only during 1993, the year that Congress chose to honor folk art. Although a variety of crafts-people were interviewed, remote galleries in the hollers of Eastern Kentucky visited, and pictures of potters and quilters at work taken, the article could be sold only once because it became obsolete in September, when most magazine editors turned their attention to January issues. "The Year of the American Craft" was over. The writer chose to accept the assignment only because the topic interested her and the price was right.

Some material may be *too local* to appeal to editors of publications outside a specific geographic area. When a talented high-school vocalist cuts her first custom album, the news is worthy of page-one treatment in her home-town's newspaper. But it's unlikely that the editor of a state or regional magazine will be interested in the story. Chances of a national sale are virtually nonexistent unless the writer recasts the material and explores a how-to angle that teaches readers how they, too, can record an album.

Some material may be *too common* to generate much enthusiasm within the editorial ranks. Living with AIDS, coping with Alzheimer's, or overcoming anorexia are topics that have been covered by most publications. Unless you have news of a medical breakthrough or a personality tie-in, you will have little chance of turning the story into multiple sales.

Other conditions that diminish an article's marketability: Your story interests too small a segment of the reading public ("How to Cope with Pregnancy After 50") or you sold all rights to the article and don't have enough material to support a "new" version.

- *You must retain the rights in an article if you hope to sell it again.*

Fortunately, most publications today buy only first rights. This means that after your article has appeared in print, you have the right to sell it again to another publication. When you approach the second editor you merely explain that the piece has been previously published and list the name(s) of the periodical(s) in which it appeared. What editors are concerned about is how many of their readers may have already seen the article in print. If the overlapping readership is limited, the editor will be more willing to run the piece. For example, if you sold an article on how to get a great suntan to a city magazine in Dayton, the identical article may also appeal to editors of city magazines in Denver, Dallas or Detroit because those magazines do not have overlapping readerships. Similarly, an article on how to plan a religious retreat would appeal to editors of other denominational periodicals even if it has already appeared in a Methodist magazine because each has a different audience. Since the second editor is buying reprint rights, he most likely will offer you less money than the first editor offered.

Occasionally an editor prefers to buy all rights. If you agree to this condition you forfeit your option to sell reprint rights. However, if the price is high enough, you may be willing to accept his terms. Some editors say they buy all rights but, when requested, they will negotiate. A writer has nothing to lose by asking.

If you sell all rights, you may still recycle the basic information in the article by creating a "new" article using the same research. This is usually not difficult, if you've done extensive research and interviewed a variety of sources. In fact, most writers are frustrated by the amount of material they have to cut to meet the word limit set by one particular editor. But for a second or third article, they can use some of the good background, statistics, and quotations they had to delete from their first version. If you began your first article with a quotation, you might begin your second with an anecdote; if you wrote the first article in third-person voice, you might write the second version from your point of view. But you must make it a new article, not just a paraphrasing of your previous article.

- *Always sell to the smallest market first; then expand to national markets.*

Create a marketing plan for your article. Offer it first to the local newspaper, and then to state, regional, national, and international publications. If you reverse the process and begin with a widely circulated national magazine, too many readers—including editors—will have seen it. The exception to this rule is in the religious marketplace. Often you can submit inspirational material simultaneously to editors of denominational magazines because circulations don't overlap.

After you've sold to a national magazine, you're not necessarily finished with your marketing efforts. You now can explore the specialty markets. Say, for example, you've written a profile of a local doctor who annually sets aside two weeks in the summer to work in a hospital in Haiti. In the course of your interview, you learn that he belongs to the Rotary Club (the Rotarians have a magazine); he's a native of Dallas (Dallas has a first-rate city magazine); he graduated from Brown University (Brown has an attractive alumni magazine); he was a member of Phi Gamma Delta collegiate fraternity (the Phi Gams publish a quarterly magazine); he was an Eagle Scout as a youth (*Scouting* magazine is always looking for appropriate articles); he attends the Nazarene church (the Nazarenes have several publications); he just turned 55 years old (would *Modern Maturity* be interested?). By changing the emphasis and playing up a certain aspect of your subject, you can produce a half-dozen articles based on the same material.

- *Never throw away a file.*

Even after you've exhausted all logical markets, hold onto your research. Why? Let's revisit the altruistic doctor who donates his time in Haiti. In five

[Sample Manuscript Submission Record]

Use a form such as this one to track the marketing and sales activity of each of your free-lance projects. By calculating the cost of producing the manuscript, you'll know how much revenue the work must generate to break even and then to make a profit. The form will be particularly helpful as you engage in multiple marketing.

Date idea was conceived _____ Date manuscript was completed _____
Time spent _____ Title _____
Length _____ Type of piece _____
Enclosures (photos, artwork, sidebars) _____

Costs:

    Research _____   Copy machine _____   Phone _____
    Travel _____   Paper _____   Disks _____
    Envelopes _____   Postage _____   Other _____

Mailed to:

Editor's name _____
Publication _____
Address _____

Date mailed _____   Date accepted/rejected _____
Editor's comments _____
_____
_____

Contractual agreements, rights, etc. _____
    Payment _____   Date received _____
    Date published _____   Profit to date _____

---

years you might want to do an anniversary update. Is he still making his annual trip? What changes has he seen over the years? What impact has his work had?

Look for other ways to recycle the material. Perhaps you're writing a round-up article about volunteerism and the doctor becomes one of five diverse people you profile as humanitarians. Or, maybe you're doing a comprehensive article on medical conditions in the Caribbean and the doctor becomes the subject of a sidebar.

The Writer and the Law

The financial drain and emotional stress that accompany legal battles are enough to give any editor, publisher or writer a headache. Unfortunately, we live in a litigation-minded society. The mindset often is, "Don't get mad, get even." And the best way to "get even" seems to be to hire an attorney and sue.

Novice writers sometimes show us their work and ask if they can be sued for something included in the manuscripts. Without hesitation we tell them that, of course, they can be sued, that a lawsuit doesn't have to have merit to be filed, and that virtually anyone can sue anyone else. However, a lawsuit doesn't imply guilt, and the plaintiff certainly may be unsuccessful in his quest for damages. The problem is that currently, regardless of a lawsuit's resolution, the defendant must hire an attorney to represent him. That costs money. Whereas a staff writer usually is covered by his employer's liability insurance policy, the free lancer is on his own.

In all matters of legal concern you should consult an attorney. But here is some general advice that may help keep you from being vulnerable to lawsuits.

Authors are usually most concerned about protecting themselves from three possible legal problems:

- Liability
- Invasion of privacy
- Libel

Liability problems may arise if a person who reads a book or article does what the writer says to do and, as a result, experiences some sort of physical, emotional or professional harm. For example, if a reader follows the advice of a book on how to purchase anatomically safe furniture and still suffers a back injury, the reader may consider the author liable and sue.

Generally speaking, the courts have not found book publishers at fault in regard to material published in their books. If the courts decide that an author did not *intentionally* recommend a product or a procedure that could harm a reader, they can be lenient. This does not mean, however, that a judge does not have the right to rule against an author. So, if you write how-to books or advice columns, be careful of what you advise people to do. Get your facts straight and double-check your findings with experts in the field.

Invasion of privacy is something journalists, interviewers, and investigative reporters are frequently accused of by people who feel their right to be left alone has been violated. Claims of invasion of privacy may occur in a variety of circumstances. Among them:

- When a person's physical solitude has been disrupted, as when an uninvited person attends a wedding or funeral just to make notes about the event, or when a photographer pushes a camera into a private automobile to take a picture of a passenger.

● When incidents in a person's private life have been exposed to public scrutiny, such as a report that claims a former army officer was medically discharged from the military when there was no reason to publicize such a matter.

● When the reporting of a person's actions puts that person in a bad light, such as saying that a woman illegally entered a private dwelling without adding that she did so to help senior citizens escape from a fire.

● When an author writes her autobiography and depicts a family member so negatively that the family member suffers a loss as a result (loss of job, reputation, position in church or community, or peace of mind).

A writer was sued for invading the privacy of a man she had never met, indeed, a man who lived more than a thousand miles from the free lancer's home. The author had been hired by a reputable publishing house to help a psychiatrist write a book about anxiety. The book included short case studies in the form of fictionalized composites of several patients. After the book was published, a former patient of the doctor claimed he recognized himself in one of the case studies and filed a multimillion-dollar lawsuit against the doctor, the publishing house, the editor, and the writer. The case dragged on for almost a year before it was settled out of court. Although the writer did not have to pay damages, the experience was costly for her. She had to hire attorneys to represent her, fly out of state to give a deposition, and spend countless hours on the telephone and in her files searching for documents related to the case.

How can such circumstances be prevented? Many writers use interview releases and photo consent forms as protection against lawsuits: If people sign these forms, they cannot claim their privacy was invaded (even if the writer says things later considered unfavorable by the subject). It is especially important to secure these release forms if sensitive material is to be taken from police or military records, medical records or school or employment records. (See samples on pages 119 and 121.)

Libel laws help protect private citizens from having unsubstantiated defamatory remarks about them appear in print or other media. A person suing an author for libel must clearly establish three facts about the author's writing: first, that the words were, indeed, defamatory; second, that the words appeared in print or were released through another communication medium (TV, radio); and third, that the person who claims to have been libeled is clearly identifiable in the context of what the writer has written.

Sometimes carelessness results in a libel suit. For example, if a writer reports that the people living at 333 Elm Street were arrested for selling drugs and, actually, it was the people living at 222 Elm Street, this could result in a libel suit. Likewise, if a writer reports that Joe Smith was expelled from college for cheating but it was actually his twin sister Jo Smith, the writer has accidentally libeled Joe. Similarly, if a criminal gives the press a fictitious name (his neighbor, his cousin, his last victim), it could make trouble for the writer unless the writer adds the qualifier "the man claimed his name was John Jones, but positive identification had not yet been established."

There have also been situations of secondary libel charges, in which a writer reports the slanderous statements of one person about another, but the writer makes no effort to determine whether or not the statements are true. If the statements prove false and do harm to the innocent party, the writer may be just as responsible as the person quoted.

Accuracy and the ability to prove whatever has been written are the best defenses against libel. Remember, too, that accuracy goes beyond stating certain facts; it also provides a correct interpretation of the situation. For example, it might be factual for you to write, "The records of Smalltown Hospital show that only two migrant workers were given proper treatment in the emergency room this summer." However, if this is true because only two migrant workers *sought* emergency room help this summer, that needs to be reported, too; otherwise, you are implying neglect or bigotry on the part of hospital personnel, and that could be interpreted as libelous.

Protection against libel suits

Should you be threatened by a libel suit and you are, indeed, guilty (unintentionally, accidentally, whatever), one of the quickest resolutions is to offer to apologize publicly and to correct the error.

Tell the person who was libeled that you are sorry and explain how the mistake was made. Promise to go to the newspaper, magazine, or TV or radio station with a retraction and correction. Do this even if you have already been served papers notifying you that you are being sued for libel. When the case comes before a judge, your retraction will serve as evidence that you meant no malice against the person claiming he was libeled. If you lose the case, the judgment may be more lenient because of your good-faith actions.

Since all writings have the potential of drawing a lawsuit, many writers like to negotiate an indemnification agreement with their publishers. Many publishers of periodicals and/or books like to insert a clause in their author contracts stating that "this author consents to indemnify and hold blameless the publisher and all of its workers, editors, representatives, distributors, and licensees against any losses, damages or incurred lawyers' fees brought on by any claim or action, suit or legal proceeding by reason of any breach by the author of any of the preceding agreements, limitations, restrictions or guidelines." Agreeing to this puts all of the legal responsibility on the

[Sample Publication Consent Agreement]

Many seasoned interviewers never bother to ask interviewees to sign formal permission forms. They feel the "unwritten" rules are clear: If a person (source) understands that a writer is gathering information for an article or book that will be published, and if that same person agrees to participate in the project by granting an interview, he or she is giving consent to the writer to use any material that comes out of the interview.

Every writer should explain, before the interview begins, that anything said during the course of the interview is "on the record," unless the interviewee clearly states otherwise. Also, the writer should explain what he or she plans to do with the information.

If you prefer to use a formal agreement, you can create a simple consent form and ask your interviewee to sign it before the start of the interview. The form might be similar to the model below.

I hereby give (*author's name*_____) the absolute right and permission to copyright and/or publish or to have copyrighted or have published the information contained about me derived from his interview with me on the below noted date. I waive any right to inspect and/or approve not only the final edited/written-for-publication versions, but also any advertising copy that may be used in connection therewith.

Date _____ **Signature** _____

Address _____

_____

Witness _____

---

shoulders of the author. If possible, it is better to get the publisher to agree to share the burden of such potential legal difficulties.

Fair comment

Among the numerous phrases and terms often tossed about in discussions of legal concern to writers is "fair comment." Fair comment is a writer's right to express an opinion about something of general interest. A travel writer may have an opinion about the service at a certain hotel, and a book reviewer may feel strongly—pro or con—about the plot and characterization in a newly released novel. These writers can publish their opinions so long as what is said is obvious to the reader as an opinion and not something that could be mistaken as research or reporting. For example, "The basketball team's center is the weak point of the squad" is the expression of a sports reporter's opinion; on the other hand, "The team's center has lost his competitive edge because of his years of substance abuse" reads like direct reporting and could, therefore, be libelous.

By choosing lives of high media visibility, public figures may be subjected to possible criticism and misstatements in the media. It goes with the territory. Although many celebrities sue periodicals for such "barbs," the courts often rule that writers who tell the truth are allowed to present a "warts and all" report about people. Public figures, according to the courts, include politicians, movie stars, best-selling authors, television personalities, and sports figures. However, people who are thrust into the limelight temporarily by a single event are not considered public figures despite the press coverage they may get for a certain amount of time (such as the winner of a $50 million state lottery or a woman who gives birth to sextuplets).

Understanding the copyright laws

The Copyright Law revision of 1978 declares that anyone who writes something—be it a travel guide or a shopping list—is the owner of that "work." Despite the simplicity of this "natural" copyrighting procedure, smart writers still need to understand some of the more formal aspects of copyrighting and possibly even consult the advice of an attorney who specializes in copyrights.

Registering a copyright to cover your work is quite simple: Call the Office of Copyrights at (202) 707-9100 and request a copyright form for the particular type of manuscript you have written. Plays require a different form from stories and articles. You can also request a variety of free brochures explaining copyright.

After filling out the form, send it along with a copy of the work (book, song, short story, photograph, poem) and a check or money order for $20 to: Publications Section, Copyright Office, Library of Congress, Washington, DC 20559. You will be sent a certificate of copyright registration. The copyright protection of your work is then valid for the duration of your life, plus 50 years (a bill before Congress at this printing seems likely to increase the duration to life plus 70 years). If a work was copyrighted during or before 1949 and renewed before the January 1, 1978, revision, the copyright was automatically extended to a total of 75 years. If it was copyrighted

[Sample Model and Photography Release Form]

In consideration for value received, receipt whereof is acknowledged, I hereby give (*author's name*_____) the absolute right and permission to copyright and/or publish, and/or resell photographic portraits or pictures of me, or in which I may be included in whole or part, for art, advertising, publicity, freelance marketing, trade or any other lawful purpose. I further extend to him/her these same rights for any photographs or portraits or related materials (brochures, programs, diaries, yearbooks, scrapbooks, albums, etc.) which I have turned over to him, including photographs I may have taken or had taken for me for my personal ownership.

I hereby waive any right that I may have to inspect and/or approve the finished product or advertising copy or related articles or photo layouts that may be used in connection therewith, or the use to which it may be applied.

I hereby release, discharge and agree to save any magazine, newspaper, newsletter or other publication that may publish these materials from any liability, including any blurring, distortion, alteration, optical illusion or use in composition form of the photographs or related materials, whether intentional or otherwise, that may occur or be produced in the making or reproducing or developing of said pictures or materials, or in any processing tending toward the completion of the finished product.

Date _____ **Signature** _____

Address _____

_____

Witness _____

between 1950 and 1978, it must be renewed to get the additional years of protection to make it 75 years of ownership for the author.

Titles, ideas, and concepts cannot be copyrighted. [Note: Writers' guilds and associations, however, will sometimes act as clearinghouses for ideas already in progress.] Small newspapers are generally not copyrighted, although a specific series or a syndicated column or special feature such as a political cartoon or a crossword puzzle may be. Magazines are usually copyrighted as entire issues; thus, if your column or article appears in that issue, it is copyrighted.

Books are usually copyrighted by the publisher, but the copyright should be in the author's name, so that if the book goes out of print all rights will revert to the author and he or she will be able to sell it elsewhere. If the book is in the publisher's name, the publisher can sell the rights without necessarily consulting the author or just hold the rights until the book goes into public domain.

The term "public domain" means that a published work does not have copyright protection, either because it was never copyrighted or the term of copyright has expired. To determine whether a work is in public domain, just subtract 75 years from the current year, and anything copyrighted that year or earlier is now in public domain. (Example: $1996 - 75 = 1921$)

If you wish to use copyrighted material in your work, you must seek the author's permission (usually by writing to the publisher or the author's agent). A payment may be required, and always an acknowledgment, for which the form will be supplied. The only time you do not need to seek permission is when the quoted material is in public domain or falls within the "fair use" context of copyright.

Four criteria guide the "fair use" limitations:

• The amount of material used cannot be a substantial section of the original work. For example, 250 words taken from a novel would be inconsequential, whereas 250 words taken from a 1,000-word article would be 25 percent of the total work. Not even two words of some lyrics can be quoted.

• The section of the material used cannot be the key passages from the work.

• Quoting this material cannot have damaging effects on the sale or earning potential of the original work.

• The use of this material in limited amounts will not be considered "commercial" if it is used for research, scholarship, news reporting, comedy, satire or parody. (See section 107 of the Copyright Act for the government's explanation of "fair use.")

Authors have the right to transfer their copyright ownership to someone else. Ownership of a specific work can be signed over to an organization or a friend or relative for tax purposes. (J. M. Barrie signed over his copyright ownership of *Peter Pan* to a British hospital. Similarly, Agatha Christie signed over the copyright of her play *The Mousetrap* to her grandson.) Copyright ownership can be transferred at death by designating a new owner in one's will. Authors can also sell all rights to a copyrighted work to a periodical or book publisher, or a vast range of subsidiary rights to a variety of buyers: movie rights to a studio, audio rights to a recording company, paperback rights to another publisher, etc. Secondary rights can be sold to a magazine that wishes to purchase excerpts from a book.

One exception to the natural copyright ownership of everything an author writes is the "work made for hire" provision in employment. If an employer, such as a newspaper or magazine or newsletter or advertising agency, hires someone to write material and pays that writer a flat fee or outright payment (or salary), the employer, not the person who wrote it, owns the writing.

When submitting a manuscript to an editor, you can state your ownership of the piece by typing the word "copyright" or its symbol ©, followed by the year the manuscript was created or copyrighted, and then the legal name (not pen name) of the person(s) who holds the copyright. (Example: © 1996 by Charles Whitney)

Type this information in the upper-right corner of the first page of an article manuscript or on the title page of a book-length manuscript.

Literary Agents: Do I Need One? How Do I Get One?

Do you need a literary agent to sell your book? Not absolutely—but there are many reasons you may want to hire one anyway.

Agents are expensive. They take a minimum of 15% of your advance payment and of future royalty earnings, and most also bill you separately for their expenses (especially photocopying costs). That's a big bite out of your income as a writer. Nevertheless, most best-selling writers really need to work through agents so that they can devote all their time to writing while the agent handles the business negotiations.

There are numerous ways to go about contacting agents. Lists of agents can be found in *The Writer's Handbook* (The Writer, Inc.), *Literary Agents of North America* (Research International, 340 E. 52nd St., New York, NY 10022), and *Literary Agents: A Writer's Guide* by Adam Begley (Poets & Writers, Inc., 72 Spring St., New York, NY 10012). You can also send $5 and a 55¢ self-addressed-stamped envelope (SASE) to the Association of Authors' Representatives, 10 Astor Pl., 3rd Fl., New York, NY 10003, and you will be sent a complete listing of the association's membership.

In order for you to determine whether or not you should seek the services of a literary agent, let's consider what an agent can and cannot do for you.

If you have an idea for a book, your agent will play devil's advocate. He'll point out any weak spots in your book proposal, help you sharpen the focus, and challenge the depth of your knowledge and research on the topic. Throughout the writing of the book the agent will boost your morale, stimulate your creativity, and serve as your confidant.

As your sales representative, the agent knows publishing trends, publishers' needs and areas of specialization. He watches publishers' ads in trade journals to determine the emphasis of each house. He knows what the range of various publishers' advances is, and when to approach a single publisher or hold an auction (open bidding) for a book.

Agents usually know when specific publishers are overstocked in certain fiction or nonfiction areas. They know which houses have the best advertising and public relations staffs, and the individual tastes and preferences of editors at various houses.

Once you've turned a completed manuscript over to an agent, he will keep it circulating among publishing houses and will prod editors to make a decision about it. When an offer is made, the agent will negotiate the contract, secure the advance check, and negotiate subsidiary rights and other benefits (serialization, foreign sales, movie rights, book club reprints, etc.). As long as the book stays in print, the agent will collect your royalties and monitor the royalty statements for accuracy.

Many agents are either lawyers or former book editors (or both). A rule of thumb often quoted in writers' circles regarding the selection of an agent is, "Remember the three R's: reputation, rates, and reception." Is the agent respected among his colleagues and peers in the publishing industry? Are his rates at the standard level for this type of work? Is he accessible to his clients and is he excited about his clients' manuscripts? Writers should ask friends and fellow writers for names of agents who are honest, experienced, creative, patient, enthusiastic, and energetic.

There are a number of tasks an agent *cannot* perform for you. Agents won't write your books or your book proposals. Many of them are not qualified to line-edit your manuscript, so they cannot serve as a syntax coach or a grammarian. They don't know any secrets that will tell you how to write a bestseller. And they personally will not advance money to you while you try to complete a book project.

It used to be that with offices right in New York, agents could call on editors and negotiate deals without much overhead. Today, however, agents have their offices all over the country and do business by fax, electronic mail, telephone, and overnight mail delivery.

Agents also must pay for office space, furniture, postage, stationery, phone bills, insurance, secretaries and staff assistants, and entertainment. Sometimes they need to hire contract consultants, copy editors, and accountants. As in all businesses, these overhead expenses can be very costly.

In seeking an agent, find out how long the agent has been in business and how many clients he or she is currently representing. Don't work with someone so overburdened you'll never get any personal attention. Ask, too, if this agent specializes in representing a certain type of writer, such as self-help authors or religion writers or business writers. Gauge the agent's savvy and intelligence, and see if the chemistry is right for a good working relationship. Keep a record of how prompt the agent is in responding to your calls and correspondence.

In contacting an agent about submitting your book proposal or completed manuscript, you need to find out first if the agent charges a reading fee. While the practice of charging a reading fee is generally frowned upon, some agents will not even look at your material unless you pay them a set hourly rate (or page rate) for examining your submission. Note: This fee provides no service to you, such as line-editing your copy or retyping your manuscript in proper format. It pays only for the agent's time. It also is no guarantee the agent will accept you as a client. Fortunately, most agents do not charge a reading fee. Furthermore, you can often meet agents face to face by attending a writers' conference where an "agent in residence" will talk to you and review your writings.

If you feel an agent may be beneficial to your career, but you are leery of binding yourself legally to someone for an extended period of time, you can hire an agent on a book-by-book basis. Just delete any self-renewing clauses in contracts and delete references to the agent's earning commissions on any free-lance sales you make on your own to newspapers and magazines. In this way, neither you nor the agent is bound to the other party without a means of terminating the arrangement.

Phase Five: Advancing Your Writing Career

Advancing Your Writing Career

"It took me fifteen years to discover I had no talent for writing, but I couldn't give it up because by that time I was too famous."
—Robert Benchley

Until now we have focused on how to improve your writing, how to recognize the various forms of free-lance writing, and how to sell what you write. Although these subjects warrant the majority of space in this book, we would be remiss if we did not touch on one more topic before concluding our text. That subject is what to do to advance yourself as a working writer once you have mastered the basics of writing and marketing.

Literally hundreds of people have approached us saying, "My dream is to work full-time as a writer." The fact is, research shows that very few writers earn a good living solely from writing. Those who do, know how to make the most of their time, talent, and opportunities. They understand the value of developing writing-related, revenue-producing skills; they are willing to promote themselves and their work; and they actively participate in a network of professional writers and editors.

In this, the final phase of our five-step program, we want to share some thoughts on how you can begin to direct yourself toward a full-time career as a writer.

Are You a *Real* Writer?

Successful writers value their time. They use and control it wisely. A young reporter once asked W. Somerset Maugham how he was able to write so many books, plays, and short stories when it was known that he wrote only from 9 a.m. until noon. Maugham responded, "I write 24 hours a day.

I *type* only three hours a day." Lesson: A real writer knows that *all* time is useful time.

To help you manage your time wisely and learn to set goals, here are some procedures to put into action:

Map out your life's goals. Philosophers refer to a person's years on earth as the "journey down the road of life." Although the expression is dull, the image is sharp. Just as you cannot drive to a previously unfamiliar destination without a detailed road map, you also cannot advance a writing career without a detailed life/career map. In both cases, you must sit down and determine your destinations. If you are contemplating a career as an author, ask yourself: "Where do I want to be a year from now? five years from now? twenty-five years from now?"

Just knowing your objective will help you reach it faster. If you want to become a best-selling novelist, set a target year for that to happen. If you want to become a syndicated columnist, decide today when you can realistically reach that goal. After making these advance decisions, you can determine what will be required to prepare for your trip to these destinations (finish a college degree? read a book a week? attend more writers' conferences?).

The "Life Map" shown on the next page will be a useful tool in helping you establish your goals as well as a time frame for accomplishing them.

Create a game plan for your 24-hour segments. Working writers leave little to chance. They do not "wing" their schedules. They list the work to be done day by day, and then systematically dig in to accomplish those objectives. By listing all the daily chores that must be handled, the individual is able to plan for blocks of time needed for big projects (doing research for a long nonfiction book) or time needed for small projects (using that last 15 minutes before lunchtime to return a call to an editor).

The sample "Daily Schedule and Planner" (see page 133) can be modified to meet your needs. Have several dozen copies run off and get into the habit of filling one out before bed each night to put into action the next day. Ten minutes of planning can save several hours of squandered time.

Set weekly, monthly, and yearly goals and write them at the top of the list as a constant reminder of the truly important objectives of your writing career. Let's say you head your list with a newspaper feature that has a Friday deadline; a national magazine article that you must finish and submit by the end of the month; and a book that must be researched by the end of the year. As you write these goals, they will become fixed in your subconscious; before long, you will find yourself directing all of your efforts toward achieving those three major goals.

Commit yourself to a time management contract. One way of making sure you

Life Map

Write a "Who's Who" entry about your life and accomplishments:

RETIREMENT

Date:
My Goal:

**Thirty Years
from Now**

Date:
My Goal:

**Fifteen Years
from Now**

Date:
My Goal:

**Five Years
from Now**

Date:
My Goal:

**Three Years
from Now**

Date:
My Goal:

**One Year
from Now**

START

Summarize your professional accomplishments to date:

Date:

don't let a year get by you without making genuine progress as a writer is to set five specific goals, write them down on a blank contract, date it, and then sign it (see page 135). Give copies to friends and ask each of them to challenge you one year later to find out how many of the goals were achieved.

Stretch yourself in selecting your goals. For example, if you read 12 books last year, make your new goal for this coming year to read 15 books. If you attended one writers' conference last year, plan to attend two this year. If you managed to write two short articles last year, make your goal to write either four articles or the first six chapters of a book.

Reduce interruptions. No writer plagued by constant interruptions can be successful. Since most free lancers write on a part-time basis and need to make every minute count, interruptions need to be controlled as much as possible.

Set and follow deadlines. In the writing business, nothing is more important than meeting the deadline. The word itself—deadline—is self-explanatory: Go past this line and you're dead! Free-lance writers must set and follow self-imposed deadlines as well as those set by editors. In writing a book for which you do not yet have a publisher, you must determine how much time you will need to complete it and then discipline yourself to stick to that time frame.

Beating a deadline is one of the best ways to impress an editor. You know how it is with bank loans: Pay off a loan one month ahead of time and you will earn an A-1 credit rating; but pay off the loan one month behind time, and you will be labeled a "bad risk" for many years to come. The same goes for writing. If you have promised to supply a magazine editor with a 2,500-word feature by June 20 and you deliver it on June 15, you will make a very favorable impression. You are trustworthy and more likely to have assignments come your way.

Identify your time sappers. One simple way to discover your time-wasting practices is to make note of everything you do for a day or two (or longer; see page 137). If it takes you 30 minutes to drive home from work, note that. If you talk on the telephone for 20 minutes, note that. If you spend a full hour at lunch, note that.

At the end of each day, tally how many hours you sat in front of the television, how much time you spent on the phone, how much time you spent waiting at offices, how long you devoted to your writing, and so on. This will show you how to turn wasted time into profitable time.

Learn to delegate work. Deciding which tasks to tackle personally and which to delegate is important. If you can pass along non-writing jobs, such as

Daily Schedule and Planner

Today's Date: _____

This Week's Goal: _____

This Month's Goal: _____

This Year's Project: _____

My Life Priorities:	Today's Errands:	Typing to Do:
	Ongoing Research Projects:	
Letters to Write:	Phone Calls to Make: / Appointments and Scheduled Interviews:	Miscellaneous:

typing or proofreading, to a competent person whom you trust to get the job done right, you will be able to devote that time to writing.

If your writing commitments are going to keep you too occupied to allow you time to accept other responsibilities, learn to say no firmly, without feeling guilty. Protect the time you will need to achieve your goals.

Abandon the "open door" policy. Fix a block of time each day for your writing and don't allow anyone to intrude. Turn on the answering machine and hang a DO NOT DISTURB sign on your door. If all this fails, find a hideout (the public library, a friend's house while she is working, your apartment complex's conference room, or a community center). You can accomplish more in two hours of privacy than in four hours with interruptions.

Control your work environment. If the activities of other members of your household distract you, keep your door closed while you are writing, or use the drone of a fan or music as "white noise" to counteract the distracting sounds.

Assemble all of your supplies before working on a project. Leaving your word processor or typewriter every ten minutes for a reference book or your note pad or your research files or a cup of coffee or your tape recorder will break your momentum in two ways: Not only will it waste valuable writing time, but it will also disrupt the intense concentration you need for the writing at hand.

Plan for a work "pause." Part-time writers who work at writing all day on weekends feel they need a half-hour coffee break in the morning and afternoon. That amounts to two wasted hours per weekend! Instead, give yourself occasional five-minute breaks for deep breathing exercises, a snack, or a brisk walk around the block. A five-minute breather is usually adequate for regenerating the creative thought processes and revitalizing your energy.

Ask yourself if you are the *only* person qualified to do a certain job. For example, if your proofreader cannot understand French and the topic of your article is "How to order from a French menu," it's up to you. Also ask yourself, "Will it take me longer to explain the job or just do it myself?" If it's a one-time job, just do it yourself. If it is repetitive, take the time to explain it once to an appropriate person and then turn it over to him or her. Finally, ask, "Does this aspect of my writing involve anything confidential?"—for instance, interview notes that you made for background information but not for publication that you alone should transcribe? If a book contract is being negotiated in a letter, perhaps a typist should not be privy to this information.

Once you delegate a task, don't oversupervise. Set a deadline for the person doing it, make regular progress checks, and never allow it to be handed back to you unfinished. For example, if you hire a college student to type the final draft of your 400-page book, tell the typist you want the

INSTRUCTIONS:

- Select five challenging activities that would improve your career and list them on your contract.

- Sign and date the contract.

- Make three copies of your contract and give one each to three close friends or business associates and ask them to challenge you on the appropriate date.

Time Management Contract

I, _____*Writer's Name*_____ , agree to accomplish each of the following items on or before _____*Target Date*_____ and thereby do formally contract myself to these purposes. These goals are challenging, but reasonable, and I accept them willingly.

(A) _____

_____

_____

(B) _____

_____

_____

(C) _____

_____

_____

(D) _____

_____

_____

(E) _____

_____

_____

Signed by: _____   Date: _____

manuscript finished in 20 days, that you will come by every five days to pick up 100 pages for proofreading, and that you will pay for the work in stages or when the entire project has been completed. Once you have the computer disk and/or the hard copy printout in hand, you'll hand over the final payment. With this arrangement, you will maintain control of the work without actually having to do it.

Maintain the momentum. A little bit of work each day will amount to a great deal of achievement during a year. If you write for a month, two hours each day from Monday through Friday, you will log a 40-hour work week on your writing career (without cutting into your eight hours of daily sleep or even interfering with your weekends). One year on that program would amount to three solid months of 40-hour work weeks. You can produce a lot of manuscript pages in that much time.

So, what are you waiting for?

Are Two Heads Better than One?

Can collaboration lead to success in writing?

You bet it can.

Can collaboration lead to failure in writing?

Can it ever!

Authors decide to work with collaborators for many reasons: Collaboration reduces the feelings of isolation and loneliness; it expands the pool of ideas and creativity; it brings on board a person who is strong in areas in which another author may be weak. It can also enhance a book's credibility factor if both authors are experts in the topic being written about. It provides motivation, feedback, and perspective. But it also has drawbacks.

If you grew up hearing such words of wisdom as, "Two heads are better than one" and "It takes two to tango," you might automatically have assumed that two writers working together would have *twice* the talent, *twice* the speed (and *twice* the royalties) as one. Not so.

Writers sometimes have personality clashes. Other times their schedules make it hard for them to work together. In yet other situations family commitments or other writing assignments or poor health or financial problems can cause one writer to be a burden rather than a blessing to a coauthorship project.

Coauthorship projects themselves can sometimes be the source of problems. One set of coauthors was asked to write a book about famous personalities who had never married. During the writing of the book some of the famous "singles" got married, new subjects had to be found and interviewed, and an end to the project never came into sight—a situation that caused friction between the coauthors.

In another situation, a writer agreed to coauthor a book with two men

The Hensley Grid

Record all activity from 8 a.m.–5:30 p.m. for a seven-day period. Tally the amount of "Unorganized" and "Organized" time on the lists below. Analyze consistent patterns or wasted time and/or effort.

	MON.	TUES.	WED.	THURS.	FRI.	SAT.	SUN.
8:00 / 8:30							
9:00 / 9:30							
10:00 / 10:30							
11:00 / 11:30							
12:00 / 12:30							
1:00 / 1:30							
2:00 / 2:30							
3:00 / 3:30							
4:00 / 4:30							
5:00 / 5:30							

Activity	Amount of Time Unorganized	Amount of Time Organized	Activity	Amount of Time Unorganized	Amount of Time Organized
Amusement	_____	_____	Sleeping	_____	_____
Civic Activities	_____	_____	Studying	_____	_____
Calling	_____	_____	Television	_____	_____
Eating	_____	_____	Thinking	_____	_____
Office Work	_____	_____	Traveling	_____	_____
Planning	_____	_____	Waiting	_____	_____
Prospecting	_____	_____	Writing	_____	_____
Religious Activities	_____	_____			

who hosted a popular radio call-in show. With the air-time exposure these two men had to publicize the book, it was thought that it would surely sell well.

Unfortunately, the writer found himself caught in a crossfire. One of his coauthors wanted the book to be sophisticated, erudite, and very intellectual, with references to aspects of psychology and psychiatry. The other author wanted the book to be filled with "street talk," pragmatic suggestions on how to get ahead in life, and a whole series of humorous anecdotes. Neither the writer nor the publisher who had commissioned the book could get the coauthors to compromise. The project was put on hold indefinitely, and the three men went their separate ways.

Yes, for a writing team to be a success, it needs a good balance of talent, marketing knowledge, discipline, cooperation, and motivation. Ironically, it also needs dashes of stubbornness, individuality, foolhardiness, and impatience.

First, you must decide what sort of collaborator you need. If you are a writer of children's books or a travel writer, you may need a collaborator who is an illustrator, graphic artist, or photographer. If you are a textbook writer, you may need the input of a research assistant or a technical writer. If you write about specialty topics, you may need an expert who is a lawyer, psychologist, accountant, or historian. If *you* are the idea person or expert, you may need to work with a published author.

Second, after you've decided what sort of person you need from a professional standpoint, make a list of the social qualities and quirks you'd like him or her to have. You might list such characteristics as honesty, integrity, good sense of humor, ability to meet deadlines, ability to accept constructive criticism, and someone who doesn't mind working early in the mornings. Remember that this person will be working with you for a long time, so make sure that you are compatible.

You can tap several outlets to find the right collaborator. Build a database (or Rolodex) of people you meet at writers' conferences, clubs, seminars, and retreats, including their names, addresses, phone numbers, and special talents. With computerized electronic mail, fax, and overnight delivery, it's possible to have a collaborator who lives far from you yet can still be your partner. Thanks to high-tech electronics, you can communicate as often as you like when working on a book project.

Check the phone book for experts in a field, as well as author and expert source directories. Also, look in a trade magazine for the names of people who are writing on topics related to your area of interest, then contact them via that magazine. Similarly, get in touch with authors of books on related topics through their publishing houses.

Third, when you make contact with a potential collaborator, try to be specific about how you envision the breakdown of work. If your first contact is by letter, you can refer to this division of duties in generalized terms, but in follow-up phone conversations, assignments should be made in specific terms.

In dividing labors, try to touch on as many areas as possible. Decide whose job it will it be to handle outlining, first drafts, revisions, interviews and research, copyediting and proofreading (of galleys, too), photography or illustration, collating chapters, photocopying, negotiating contracts, typing, record keeping and accounting, publicity, technical verifications, indexing, copyright filing, and mailing.

Sometimes collaborators have overlapping responsibilities when it comes to writing, editing, typing, and proofreading. One of you handles publicity (book-signing requests, talk-show appearances, phone interviews, dust-jacket copy, publicity photos), while the other handles the business matters (contract negotiations, workshop bookings, transportation, expense accounts). In this way you can work on a variety of important tasks simultaneously.

It's also best for coauthors to have a signed agreement covering how royalties and expenses will be shared, how bylines will be listed, and other business matters will be handled. In this way, if something drastic happens— like one partner's illness—procedures will already be in place for carrying projects forward.

Having settled on *whom* to write with, the next challenge is to learn *how* to write with someone. The key to a successful collaboration is to have a specific system for working together. For example, two writers who specialize in books on health care follow a set procedure. They first sit down and create a rough outline. One writer decides what the key topics of the chapters will be and the other writer suggests the research material that should be used for those topics. Once they are satisfied with the outline, they divide the chapters and get to work.

After one writer finishes the first chapter, he sends it to his coauthor. He might also send a follow-up cassette in which he talks about elements of the research, new interview sources, and possible sidebar material. The coauthor then gives the chapter a thorough editing. He adds paragraphs of research data, more quotations from expert sources, and possibly an anecdote to illustrate a point. When done, the chapter has a style that is neither one writer's nor the other's, but is a unique third voice. The process reverses as the second writer writes a chapter and sends it to the first writer for revisions and additions.

Here are some suggestions for maintaining a successful coauthorship arrangement:

● Work with someone who is your equal in talent and skill. If you respect each other's abilities, you'll be more apt to accept suggestions, critiques, and revisions from one another.

- Don't work with a clone of yourself. Find someone who has a different set of experiences to bring to your collaboration. For example, people with different backgrounds and work histories can complement each other. Perhaps one partner is a paralegal who earned her degree at night school in Kalamazoo while working days as a librarian. Her partner might be a gift shop owner who grew up in Atlanta and has also been a naval cadet. All of these experiences can be beneficial in selecting and researching topics.

- Find someone who is strong in your areas of weakness. One partner may have had a lot of formal training in the technical aspects of writing and thus would be good at editing and proofreading. The other partner may have spent years as a research assistant and is good at obtaining data for articles and books.

- Divide everything equally. We receive 50-50 shares of advance money and royalties on our books, and our publishers send us separate checks. We seldom touch each other's money.

- Choose a hard worker. Each partner must do his or her half of the writing, must meet deadlines, and must be available to make appearances on TV and radio talk shows to publicize the finished books.

- Develop a tough skin. Be sure you and your collaborator listen to each other and make whatever changes are needed, no matter how much has to be cut or rewritten. You both should want a quality product and be willing to do whatever it takes to obtain that goal.

Spinoff Activities: Workshops and Other Sidelines

Most writers cultivate a variety of writing-related sidelines. Some teach college classes, some lead writers' workshops, some do free-lance editing, and some serve as consultants for companies that want to improve their in-house publications or need annual reports and speeches written. All this is done *in addition to* the primary writing duties.

Why would a serious author take on such a variety of odd jobs? For one reason: stability.

A free lancer doesn't have the luxury of a regular salary. Checks sometimes arrive in flurries and are followed by long dry spells. Even a generous book advance wears thin when stretched over several months. Teaching a night class at the local college may add only a few hundred dollars to your income, but the payments are regular and will keep you in coffee, diskettes, and other staples.

However, homebound writers also crave another kind of stability—emotional stability. Without the camaraderie of office colleagues, a writer who works out of her home can become too much of a loner. Uninterrupted days at the keyboard may sound like glorious solitude, but in reality, they can be stressful. Depression brought on by rejection is another occupational hazard. Writing-related activities that allow the author to leave her keyboard and mix with others who share her interests help her relieve the stress and combat the blues.

The ideal situation is an activity that provides both financial and emotional stability. Leading a writers' workshop or consulting with a local business would be just such an opportunity.

Building a portfolio

The range of spinoff activities available to you as a writer depends on your interests, your abilities, and your clips. Start to assemble a portfolio as soon as you earn your first byline, not to exhibit every piece of writing you have ever done, but to offer a sampling of your best work. The album becomes a sales tool as you go in search of spinoff assignments. The looseleaf pages enable you to rearrange and substitute clips, depending on their relationship to the assignment you seek.

An impressive portfolio can have a real impact on a corporate client who is less impressed by what you *say* you can do, than by what you've already done. Clips are tangible evidence of your talents.

As you approach local companies and organizations, be aware of those that are cutting staff or use outside consultants to write their annual reports, news releases, or employee newsletters. If an organization is gearing up to celebrate a special anniversary (centennial, 50th, or 25th year in business), propose a company history or some other commemorative piece for distribution to employees, customers, the community, and the media. Such an assignment will not only earn you a sizable fee, but it will also make a good addition to your growing portfolio.

Sharing your knowledge

Although you need a minimum of a master's degree to teach for a college or university, you need no special schooling to teach in a continuing education program. People who enroll in noncredit classes are far more interested in an instructor's experience than in her formal education. If you are a published author, you have the credibility to teach would-be writers how to break into print. Continuing education classes usually meet in the evening, run from one to three hours, are informal and friendly, and lack the structure imposed by textbooks, tests, or grades. The direction of the course is determined by the interests of the teacher and her students.

As your bylines mount, and as you become more and more comfortable in front of a group, you may want to try your hand at leading workshops. Hundreds of writing seminars are conducted every year across the country and each requires several speakers. Some seminars are very specialized and reach out to those who want to write mysteries, romance, humor, or travel material. Other workshops are general and offer sessions in nonfiction, fiction, poetry, and scriptwriting.

The best way to become a regular on the workshop circuit is to send your credentials to a variety of workshop directors, whose names and addresses are listed in the spring issues of most writers' magazines. The faculty of a workshop is usually recruited six months to a year before the dates of the conference, so make your contacts early. Arrangements usually include travel expenses, room, board, and an honorarium of from $500 to $1,000. Some workshops last for a day, others may continue for a week or two. A bonus is the "book table" that allows speakers to place their books on sale to conference participants. The workshop may have a policy that specifies that the sponsoring organization keeps 10% to 25% of book sales.

Before hiring you to teach at their seminars, directors want to know what and where you have published, your experience as a seminar speaker, a list of topics you are qualified to address, one or two references, and possibly an audiotape of a workshop you've given. They may also inquire as to your willingness to critique manuscripts and meet one-on-one with conferees.

Publicizing You and Your Work

Unless you are an established author with a solid track record for generating sales, most publishing companies won't budget large sums for the promotion of your book. In the case of small publishers—university and religious presses among them—the funds are simply not available. So, you ought to set aside time to promote and publicize your work on your own. You can do so without spending a great deal of money.

Start by generating free publicity. Send information about yourself and your newly released book to the alumni news section of your college/university magazine and newspaper. Put announcements in your neighborhood association newsletters, your church bulletin and your writers' club news notes. Make a list of every affiliation you have—college fraternity or sorority, service clubs, honorary societies, professional associations—and send each one an announcement and current photograph of yourself and the book.

Send your publisher a list of newspapers and magazines where you feel review copies of your book should be directed. If you have been a frequent contributor to a certain magazine, the editor of that publication is another likely recipient of a copy of your book. As part of your contract negotiations, ask for an adequate supply of complimentary copies (contracts typically stipulate that six to 10 books go to the author) so you can send your book to media editors you know personally. Boost your chances of getting your books reviewed by remembering these four points:

- Critics for newspapers or general-interest magazines prefer to review works of fiction, politics, history, biography, or contemporary issues and events. Specialty magazines are more inclined to review books about specialty topics: gardening, art, music, diets, and self-help topics.

• Reviewers are far more likely to pay attention to a book published by a major publisher; so, try to sign with the best publisher possible.

• Since the fame and reputation of an author will convince reviewers they should review his or her book, generate as much publicity for yourself and your book as you can.

• If your book has any regional appeal, contact the newspapers in that area to start the publicity momentum.

Alert service clubs and private organizations on both the local and national level (Rotary, VFW, Elks, etc.) of your willingness to address them regarding the topic of your book. On the day of the speech, set up a library table where you can sell and autograph copies of your book. If your book focuses on a theme or cause of concern to a national organization, try to obtain a formal endorsement from that organization. For example, when Jonellen Heckler wrote *A Fragile Peace*, a novel about the problems of alcoholism in a family, she was able to secure an endorsement from Alcoholics Anonymous, which cited the book as recommended reading for anyone who wanted to learn more about how to deal with alcoholism.

Along that same line, if you can, obtain endorsement quotations from experts or noted authorities or personalities—your publisher may be able to make use of them in ads for your book or to print on the dust jacket. You might also help promote your book at book fairs or conventions your publisher will be attending.

Visit your area bookstores and show a copy of your book to the managers. If they suggest an autograph party, you may be asked to supply a list of friends and associates to be included on the invitation list. Contrary to popular belief, people don't flock to a bookstore to attend an autograph party. They have to be wooed in. Anything you can do to ensure success will be appreciated . . . and remembered. If this first party is a success, you will find it much easier to schedule another party at the same store when your next book is published.

Tell your publisher that you are willing to appear as a guest on radio and television talk shows. Many radio interviews can be conducted by phone from your home or office.

Although your publishing house may not be willing to underwrite a national publicity tour, it may be willing to arrange media interviews for you when you are on the road. Be sure to alert your publisher of your travel plans for business trips and holidays. Coordinate your travel with bookings in those cities for talk-show appearances and newspaper interviews. Keep in mind that the most successful way to sell any product is word of mouth.

Do everything you can to encourage people to read and talk about your book.

Building a Network for Success

A first sale is usually the result of talent and timing. An unsolicited manuscript arrives at the editorial offices of a magazine and is so clever, so well written, and so perfectly targeted to the readers of the publication that the editors simply have to find a place for it. That's talent.

Timing is also very important. Knowing what editors are looking for and delivering a manuscript that fills their needs at precisely the right moment to meet their deadline almost ensures publication.

Although talent and timing may help you achieve your first byline, networking keeps you in print on a regular basis. By definition, networking is knowing editors and publishers well enough to participate in ongoing, two-way communication with them. When you are part of the publishing network, editors contact you as often as you contact them. You no longer blindly send out queries and manuscripts hoping you might hit a magazine staff's hot button with one of your ideas. The process is reversed. Editors let you know what they are looking for and tell you what assignments are up for grabs. They may put you on their complimentary subscription list or even put you on their masthead as a contributing editor. Indirectly, this can translate into money. You won't be on the payroll, but you may earn a higher rate of payment when one of your submissions is accepted for publication.

How do you become a member of the network? It doesn't happen quickly and it requires a great deal of continuous work. Here are several pointers:

Strike a match. For starters, you must decide on the editors with whom you want to establish a relationship; then it's up to you to make the initial contact by mail. Too often free lancers get in touch with editors only when they are asking for guidelines or trying to sell an idea, proposal, or manuscript. Try a different approach. Send an editor a friendly letter of introduction, include a couple of your best clips and a business card, mention any areas of expertise you have, and invite the editor to keep you in mind for future assignments in your part of the country. Remember, editors are always looking for fresh, strong voices for inclusion in their magazines. Your challenge is to speak up.

Keep in touch. After you've made a contact, update an editor on what's happening professionally in your life that could benefit his publication. For example, inform editors of any trips you have planned. This is important for two reasons: Editors will know why you aren't returning phone messages if they are trying to reach you; and they may have a story that they would like you to pursue while you're on the road.

Make editors aware of any new topics you've researched, new experiences you've had, and new skills you've acquired. If you've taken up photography, send them a sample picture for inclusion in your file. If you've always written health and fitness articles but have recently attended a workshop on travel writing, let them know of your willingness to tackle a travel assignment. Always correspond in such a way that the editors don't have to reply if they have nothing to say. After all, editors want professional associates, not pen pals.

Say what you think, do what you're told. Editors need sounding boards. They like to bounce ideas off objective people who are not afraid to speak up—people who have different points of view and who represent a cross section of the country. They appreciate colleagues who will give them honest feedback. However, writers get in trouble when they think they know more than editors. The wise free lancer will offer his opinion on an issue *once,* then, if overruled, accept the editor's decision.

Be willing to take an assignment you may not enjoy. One journalist we know has written many celebrity profiles and is often asked to list her favorite subjects. George Burns? Dear Abby? Cartoonist Jim Davis and Garfield? Dolly Parton? Seldom is she asked about the uncomfortable interviews: the Milwaukee grandfather who contracted AIDS from a tainted blood transfusion; Jill Ireland right before her death from cancer; Annette Funicello shortly after she was diagnosed with multiple sclerosis.

Editors appreciate writers who understand that all assignments aren't going to be easy or fun or glamorous. As a trusted member of the publishing network, you need to build a reputation as a writer who is willing to write about anything. Editors often show their gratitude by alternating tough assignments with enjoyable ones for regular contributors who have earned their stripes.

Understand an editor's job. Believe it or not, editors are human, are overworked, and as a consequence, are capable of making mistakes—sometimes at a free lancer's expense. We've heard of instances in which a free lancer's byline has been misspelled or, worse yet, omitted. Occasionally paragraphs are cut from articles and transitions no longer make sense. Sometimes key numbers are transposed, making the information in an article inaccurate. Errors such as these reflect badly on the writer, the editor, and the publication.

Often the free lancer's first inclination is to call mistakes to the attention of the editor and request a correction in the next issue of the publication. But for what purpose? The damage is done, the story is in print, and the issue is on the newsstand. The better course of action is to understand that mistakes are usually oversights and are committed under the stress of deadlines. The smart free lancer merely writes a note, thanks the editor for the opportunity to write for the publication, and expresses interest in future assignments.

Acquire networking tools. In the current age of entrepreneurship, launching a business as a serious free lancer is relatively inexpensive. Your equipment needs are as simple as a telephone, typewriter, perhaps a tape recorder, a supply of envelopes, and assorted postage. However, active members of the publishing network have more sophisticated requirements. Editors rarely depend solely on the U.S. mail to communicate with their trusted writers. Initial contacts are made by phone; consequently, an active free lancer needs either an answering machine or voice mail service to ensure that no calls are lost. Letters of assignment and article guidelines may be transmitted and confirmed by fax to cut down on time. Finished articles may be submitted on disk, by fax, or by electronic mail. The free lancer who has access to these communication devices removes barriers erected by time and space.

Many beginning writers think they must invest large amounts of money in expensive equipment before they can succeed in the free-lance business. This simply is not true. Writers should create a list of equipment needs and organize the list by priority. As sales become more frequent, they should begin to purchase equipment that will help them be more efficient in their work and more accessible to editors.

No electronic gizmo can disguise or improve poor writing. Manuscripts can look like works of art, thanks to computers and laser printers that offer a variety of fonts and options such as justified margins, oversized titles, italicized and boldface type. Submissions can arrive at an editor's desk with an air of importance provided by electronic mail, overnight delivery, or fax transmission. However, the value of an article, story or book is determined solely by its words. Work first on your words and worry later about presentation and enhancements.

Only then will you be an author who consistently writes on target.

Glossary

Advance—An amount paid to an author by a publisher before a book is published; it is deducted from the royalties earned from sales after the book is on the market (advance against royalties).

Agent *also* **author's representative**—A person or agency that submits an author's manuscripts to publishers, negotiates contracts, monitors royalty payments, and serves as buffer between writer and publisher. Paid a percentage of the earnings from sales of a book.

All rights—Permanent ownership of creative material obtained from an author by a publisher.

Anecdote—A short account of a humorous or interesting incident used to illustrate a key point; often serves as the lead into an article.

Assignment—A written or oral contract between an editor and writer that confirms that the writer will complete a specific project by a certain date and for a certain fee.

As-told-to article/book—Nonfiction collaborative work in which one person's story is written by another person.

Attribution—Identification of the source of information. Can be done either by direct quote ("I like criticism, but it must be my way," said Mark Twain) or by paraphrase (Robert Frost always said that a person could be a little ungrammatical if he came from the right part of the country).

B&W—Editor's jargon for black-and-white photographs.

Bio note—Short blurb that tells a few pertinent facts about the author of an article.

Blue pencil—To edit a manuscript, i.e., "the editor blue-penciled the article."

Blurb—Short description of a book or an author; often appears on a dustjacket.

Body—The dominant portion of an article; follows the lead and precedes the conclusion.

Book outline—Chapter-by-chapter summary, often written in paragraph form, that allows an editor to evaluate the content and pacing of a book.

Book proposal—A multi-part package that contains a cover letter, synopsis, table of contents, outline and sample chapters.

Byline—Author's name, usually printed below title and above text.

Caption—Description of a photograph's content; also called cutlines by many newspaper editors.

Clips—Tear sheets or copies of a writer's published works; often requested by editors who want to evaluate a potential contributor's talent.

Closing date—Deadline for editorial and advertising copy for a particular issue of a publication.

Coauthorship—The collaboration between two or more writers.

Column inch—A unit of measurement that often serves as a basis for payment. A column inch is always one inch in depth; however, width varies according to the publication's established format.

Contributor's copies—Copies of a publication sent to writers whose works are included in a magazine.

Copublishing—Agreement between a writer and publisher to split the costs and profits of publication.

Copy—Manuscript pages before they are set into type.

Copy editing—Line-by-line editing to ensure correct spelling, grammar, punctuation and consistent style; not to be confused with content editing, which scrutinizes flow, logic, and overall message.

Copyright—Legal protection of published and unpublished creative works from unauthorized use.

Cover letter—An introductory letter that accompanies a manuscript or a book proposal.

Coverline—Short phrase printed on the cover of a magazine to promote an article within the issue.

Correspondent—Writer who works from his home and produces material for a newspaper on an assignment basis; sometimes called a stringer.

Credit line—Designates the photographer or illustrator who is responsible for a piece of published art work; similar to a writer's byline.

Credits sheet—Listing of periodicals in which an author has been published. Book publishers sometimes request credits sheets before deciding to issue contracts to unknown writers.

Critique—An evaluation of a manuscript; often addresses the marketability of the material.

Crossover material—Appeals to more than one market or audience; often used to describe inspirational material that attracts secular and religious readers.

Deadline—A date agreed to by author and editor on which a written work is due at the editor's office.

Demographics—Vital statistics of a publication's readers; i.e., the age, education level, income, gender, and geographic location of the readers.

Documentation—Proof, support, or evidence for a general statement or idea; often takes the form of statistics, quotations, and examples. In a scholarly work, documentation may refer to footnotes and endnotes that show the source of certain material.

Draft—A single, complete version of an article or book. First drafts frequently are called rough drafts.

Editorial—Opinion piece, often written by a member of a publication's staff, that attempts to influence or persuade readers.

Essay—Narrative piece of writing that represents the author's point of view on a certain topic.

Expository article—A piece of writing whose main purpose is to explain.

Fair use—Part of the copyright law that permits brief passages of copyrighted material to be quoted without fear of infringing on the owner's rights.

Feature—An article that usually is not time-dated, often is longer than a news story, and focuses on an issue, trend, or person.

Filler—Brief item often used to surprise or amuse readers. Puzzles and anecdotes qualify as fillers.

First-person article—Written from author's point of view; many magazines have firm policies regarding first-person material and actively solicit or routinely reject such submissions.

First rights—The right to publish a creative work first; after publication, the rights are returned to the author.

Five W's and the H—Elements of a summary lead that answer the questions: who, what, where, when, why and how?

Format—The way a publication or an article within a publication is laid out and designed.

Free lancer—A writer who is not on the staff of a publication but sells manuscripts to a variety of editors on speculation or on assignment.

Frontlist—New books promoted in a publishing house's recent catalogue.

Gag line—A cartoon's caption; also, the punch line inside a humorous greeting card.

Gang query—A letter sent by a free lancer to an editor pitching two or more ideas for magazine articles.

Ghostwriter—"Anonymous" author who produces books, articles, and speeches that are credited to someone else.

Glossy—Black-and-white photo that has a shiny, rather than a matte, finish.

Hitch-hiker feature—Article that is related to a newsworthy topic and becomes timely by association. Example: Sexual harassment in the workplace became the subject of numerous books and articles after Anita Hill's accusations against Supreme Court nominee Clarence Thomas. The topic "hitch-hiked" into prominence by way of a national incident.

Honorarium—A flat fee (often a token amount) paid by a publication to an author in gratitude for a submission.

Hook—Lead or introductory paragraph designed to grab the reader's attention.

Hotbox—An offshoot of an article, usually fewer than 100 words, that is set off from the main article and placed in a box with a separate title.

How-to article—Article that offers step-by-step instruction or advice on a process to create a product or bring about a change.

International postal reply coupon—Available at the post office and included with any correspondence to a foreign publication; allows the editor to reply without incurring cost.

Inverted pyramid—Traditional organization of a newspaper article; pertinent information is placed at the "top" of the story, and additional material is arranged in an order of descending importance.

Kill fee—Amount of money paid to a writer who completes an assignment that is not published by the periodical that made the assignment; usually a percentage of the dollar amount that would have been paid had the work been published.

Lead—The opening sentence of a story or article; should attract readers' attention and make them want to continue reading.

Libel—Legal term for published a false statement that causes a person embarrassment, loss of income, or damage to reputation.

Little magazines—Publications that are highly respected although their circulations are small; content often deals with literature or politics.

MS—Accepted abbreviation for manuscript; mss is the abbreviation for more than one manuscript.

Mass market—Book not targeted to a specialized audience; appeals to very large segment of the reading public.

Masthead—A listing of the names and titles of the publication's staff members.

Multiple marketing—Systematic recycling of free-lance material to different publications.

Multiple submissions—Identical manuscripts sent simultaneously to different publications.

Net to author—Cash amount paid to a book author and based on the contract between writer and publisher; may vary from 10 percent of the wholesale price to 10 percent of the retail price.

News article—Often arranged in the inverted pyramid style, designed to convey information clearly and quickly.

News peg—Factor that makes a piece timely; ties a free-lance article to something timely in the news.

Off the record—Information shared with the understanding that it will not be used in print.

On acceptance—Payment to writer when manuscript is submitted.

On publication—Payment to writer when work appears in print.

On speculation—Writer submits work to an editor without any assurance that the editor will purchase the work.

One-time rights—Editor purchases work from an author and agrees to publish it one time. After the work has appeared in print, the rights to the work revert to the author for subsequent sales.

Op-Ed—Newspaper page devoted to opinion material and editorials; often includes a guest column open to readers who want to speak out on an issue. Appears opposite the editorial pages.

Outline—The skeleton or summary of an article or book; indicates content, flow, transitions, and pacing.

Over-the-transom manuscript—Unsolicited manuscript; expression is a throwback to the days when mail carriers heaved envelopes up and through the small open windows (transoms) above office doors.

Page rate—Manner by which some editors purchase material for publication; refers to a set fee that "buys" enough words to fill one magazine page.

Pen name—Also called pseudonym, the name other than an author's legal name that appears on his/her written work.

Personal-experience story—An account of an actual happening, written from the author's point of view.

Personality profile—An article that focuses on one person's character, contributions, talents, fame.

Photo feature—A series of photographs that tells a story; usually accompanied by captions or short blocks of text.

Photocopied submission—Manuscript that has been reproduced on a copy machine and submitted to an editor for consideration; most publications no longer insist on receiving the original manuscript.

Public domain—Written material not covered under the copyright law; available for public use without permission.

Proposal—A complete outline of a project with one or two sample chapters.

Q-and-A format—Popular presentation of an interview article; questions are stated, followed by verbatim answers from the interviewee.

Query—A letter that proposes an article idea to an editor; usually no longer than a page.

Rejection slip—A printed note stating a publication is not interested in a manuscript submission.

Reporting time—The days (or weeks) required for an editor to evaluate a submission.

Reprint rights—The legal right of an editor to reprint an article or story that has been published previously.

Rough draft—The first complete copy of a manuscript; subsequent drafts will refine the rough copy.

Round-up article—A piece in which the author selects a common topic or theme and gathers several perspectives on it. Example: "The 10 Best Theme Parks in the USA."

Royalty—A percentage of the amount received from sales of a book, paid to the author by the book publisher.

SASE—Self-addressed, stamped envelope.

Self-publish—Publication of a work by the author, rather than by a commercial publishing company, and paid for by the author.

Serial—Publication that is printed and distributed on a regular schedule, such as a newspaper or magazine.

Sidebar—A short article that accompanies and relates to a major feature and presents a different angle on the subject. (See also *hotbox.*)

Simultaneous submission—Submission of a manuscript to several publishers at the same time.

Slice of life—A scene that captures a moment in time; it doesn't tell a complete story but can make a point.

Slides—Color transparencies, often preferred by editors.

Slush—Unsolicited manuscripts that flood every editorial office.

Staff-written features—Columns, departments, and other regular magazine features that are written by full-time members of the publication's staff.

Standing feature—A column that is published in every issue of a periodical.

Stringer—A non-salaried member of a newspaper's staff who occasionally covers an event.

Subsidiary rights—All rights, other than standard book-publishing rights, that are covered in a book contract; may include film, paperback and book-club rights.

Subsidy publisher—A publishing company that charges an author all costs of printing a book; sometimes called a vanity press.

Syndication rights—Rights purchased by a newspaper syndicate authorizing the syndicate to print a book (in installments) or a column in one or more newspapers.

Tabloid—Newspaper about half the size of a standard newspaper. Examples: *The National Enquirer, Newsday.*

Takeaway value—The lesson in an article or book that readers can take with them and apply in their personal lives.

Tear sheet—Magazine pages(s) on which an author's work is published.

Think piece—A magazine or newspaper article that deals with an important issue in a thought-provoking and philosophical manner.

Tone—An author's manner in discussing a topic; tones can be formal, chatty, sarcastic, witty, etc.

Trade publication—Magazine whose readers share a specific profession or business, with editorial material related to the technical aspects of the business.

Unsolicited manuscripts—Poetry, short stories, articles, books that arrive unannounced and unrequested at editorial offices.

Well—Center section of a magazine; generally contains color photos and the issue's major articles.

Work for hire—Clause in a signed agreement that gives all rights to the company that publishes a piece of work.

Writer's guidelines—A publication's editorial needs, payment schedule, deadlines, and other essential information.